VOGUE KNITTING
VESTS

VOGUE KNITTING
VESTS

SOHO PUBLISHING COMPANY
NEW YORK

SOHO PUBLISHING COMPANY
233 Spring Street
New York, New York 10013

Library of Congress Cataloging-in-Publication Data

Vogue knitting vests.
     p. cm. -- (Vogue knitting on the go!)
    ISBN 1-931543-08-9
    1. Knitting--Patterns. 2. Vests. I. Title: Vests. II. Malcolm,
Trisha, 1960- III. Series.

  TT825 .V6487 2002
  746.43'20432--dc21   2001049629

Manufactured in China

1 3 5 7 9 10 8 6 4 2

First Edition

TABLE OF CONTENTS

INTRODUCTION

In the midst of a hectic day, what could be more soothing than the reassuring rhythm of clicking needles and the sensation of yarn running through your fingers? If your too-busy schedule has led you to believe there's no time in your day for a pleasure as simple as knitting, think again. In an age of instant access, express service, and unstable markets, there's one investment you'll never regret making: a little time, each day, for yourself and the craft you love. The payoff? A moment to relax, a chance to surrender to the lullaby of knitting, and a beautiful product for yourself or a loved one.

The vests in this book have been created with these ends in mind. Each project is designed to capitalize on color, texture, and above all, the moments in each day—perhaps on the train, on a lunch break, or during a favorite TV show—that can be devoted to a few rows of knitting. Whether knitting for yourself, your spouse, your child, or a friend, you'll find much inspiration within these pages. Best of all, after knitting just two or three pieces, you'll have a complete garment!

Use the designs in this book as springboards for your imagination. Try experimenting with different yarns (just be sure to check your gauge first), stitch patterns, and color combinations. Speed up the process by working with chunky or doubled-stranded yarn. Examine your favorite sweater patterns—they'll be whole new looks without sleeves. Try them long or short, flowing or fitted—what great outfit can't be made better with a vest?

Time may be precious, but vests are timeless. You owe it to yourself to set aside a little time to **KNIT ON THE GO!**

THE BASICS

From the boardroom to the playroom, from power lunches to weekend escapes in the country, vests have a place in everyone's wardrobe. With the same ease that they crisply top off a classic shirt and tie, vests can offer a bit of whimsy or flair to almost any outfit. Like the people who wear them, each vest in this book is unique and offers an opportunity to express a touch of personal style. Does the orderly symmetry of the Traditional Man's Vest (page 78) suit your stock-trading brother, or is he the kind of guy to wear the Man's Tweed Vest (page 82)? Is the soft, feminine Diamond Lace Vest (page 52) a perfect fit for your mother, or would she prefer the classic chic of the Checked Pullover (page 59)? Do you envision yourself on a brisk fall walk wearing a cozy Hooded Vest (page 46) or making a bold statement in a bright Bi-color Vest (page 36)? There's something here for all ages, all occasions, and all styles.

Vests are excellent choices for knitters with little time to spare: there are no time-consuming sleeves to knit, and many designs require minimal finishing. Still, they present endless opportunities for creativity. Cable, lace, and color patterns abound, and details such as hoods, pockets, zippered fronts, belts, contrasting trims, and even buttons pop out as eye-catching design elements. Because vests require significantly less yarn than full-sized pullovers and cardigans, you may feel inclined to splurge on a high-end or luxury yarn. Or, you may be inspired to mix and match yarns from your stash for a creation that is uniquely your own.

SIZING

When determining what size vest to make, measure a sweater that fits you well, then compare these measurements to those given in the "Knitted Measurements" section of the pattern.

GARMENT CONSTRUCTION

Aside from the traditional ways of knitting pieces and sewing them together, we have explored some more unusual techniques of sample making. The Man's Fair Isle Vest (page 24) is worked entirely in the round, using the steek method of cutting stitches for the armhole and neck opening. Sewing with chunky yarns can make a thick seam; therefore, eliminating seams is always advisable. Even though most of the garments in this book are made in pieces, if you are a fairly experienced knitter, you can try knitting many of them in the round to the underarm—you just need to make some simple adjustments to the pattern.

YARN SELECTION

For an exact reproduction of the projects photographed, use the yarn listed in the "Materials" section of the pattern. We've chosen yarns that are readily available in the U.S. and Canada at the time of printing. The Resources list on pages 94 and 95 provides addresses of yarn distributors. Contact them for the name of a retailer in your area.

GAUGE

It is always important to knit a gauge swatch, and it is even more so with garments to ensure proper fit.

Patterns usually state gauge over a 4"/10cm span; however, it's beneficial to make a larger test swatch. This gives you a more precise stitch gauge, a better idea of the appearance and drape of the knitted fabric, and a chance to familiarize yourself with the stitch pattern.

The type of needles used—straight or circular, wood or metal—will influence gauge, so knit your swatch with the needles you plan to use for the project. Measure gauge as illustrated. Try different needle sizes until your sample measures the required number of stitches and rows. *To get fewer stitches to the inch/cm, use larger needles; to get more stitches to the inch/cm, use smaller needles.*

Knitting in the round may tighten the gauge, so if you measured the gauge on a flat swatch, take another gauge reading after you begin knitting. When the piece measures at least 2"/5cm, lay it flat and measure over the stitches in the center of the piece, as the side stitches may be distorted.

It's a good idea to keep your gauge swatch in order to test blocking and cleaning methods.

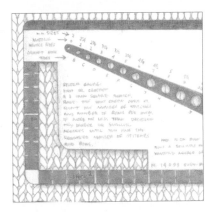

YARN SUBSTITUTION

You may wish to substitute yarns. Perhaps you view small-scale projects as a chance to incorporate leftovers from your yarn stash, or the yarn specified may not be available in your area. You'll need to knit to the given gauge to obtain the knitted measurements with a substitute yarn (see "Gauge" above). Be sure to consider how the fiber content of the substitute yarn will affect the comfort and the ease of care of your projects.

To facilitate yarn substitution, *Vogue Knitting* grades yarn by the standard stitch gauge obtained in stockinette stitch. You'll find a grading number in the "Materials" section of the pattern, immediately following the fiber type of the yarn. Look for a substitute yarn that falls into the same category. The suggested needle size and gauge on the yarn label should be comparable to that on the Yarn Symbols chart (see page 13).

After you've successfully gauge-swatched a substitute yarn, you'll need to figure out how much of the substitute yarn the project requires. First, find the total length of the original yarn in the pattern (multiply number of balls by yards/meters per ball). Divide this figure by the new yards/meters per ball (listed on the yarn label). Round up to the next whole number. The answer is the number of balls required.

FOLLOWING CHARTS

Charts are a convenient way to follow colorwork, lace, cable, and other stitch patterns at a glance. *Vogue Knitting* stitch charts utilize the universal knitting language of "symbolcraft." When knitting back and forth in rows, read charts from right to left on right side (RS) rows and from left to right on wrong side (WS) rows, repeating any stitch and row repeats as directed in the pattern. When knitting in the round, read charts from right to left on every round. Posting a self-adhesive note under your working row is an easy way to keep track of your place on a chart.

COLORWORK KNITTING

Two main types of colorwork are explored in this book.

Intarsia

Intarsia is accomplished with separate bobbins of individual colors. This method is ideal for large blocks of color or for motifs that aren't repeated close together. When changing colors, always pick up the new color and wrap it around the old color to prevent holes.

For smaller areas of color, such as the accent snowflakes on the Christmas Vest

(page 90), duplicate stitch embroidery is done after the pieces are knit.

Stranding

When motifs are closely placed, colorwork is accomplished by stranding along two or more colors per row, creating "floats" on the wrong side of the fabric. This technique is sometimes called Fair Isle knitting after the traditional Fair Isle patterns that are composed of small motifs with frequent color changes.

To keep an even tension and prevent holes while knitting, pick up yarns alternately over and under one another across or around. While knitting, stretch the stitches on the needle slightly wider than the length of the float at the back to keep work from puckering.

When changing colors at the beginning of rows or rounds, carry yarn along for a few rows only, or cut yarn and rejoin when needed. It is important to keep the floats small and neat so they don't catch when pulling on the piece.

BLOCKING

Blocking is an all-important finishing step in the knitting process. It is the best way to shape pattern pieces and smooth knitted edges in preparation for sewing together. Most garments retain their shape if the blocking stages in the instructions are followed carefully. Choose a blocking method according the the yarn care label and when in doubt, test-block your gauge swatch.

Wet Block Method

Using rust-proof pins, pin pieces to measurements on a flat surface and lightly dampen using a spray bottle. Allow to dry before removing pins.

Steam Block Method

With WS facing, pin pieces. Steam lightly,

YARN SYMBOLS

① **Fine Weight**
(29-32 stitches per 4"/10cm)
Includes baby and fingering yarns, and some of the heavier crochet cottons. The range of needle sizes is 0-4 (2-3.5mm).

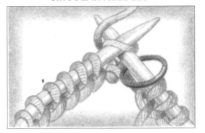

Hold the needle tip with the last cast-on stitch in your right hand and the tip with the first cast-on stitch in your left hand. Knit the first cast-on stitch, pulling the yarn tight to avoid a gap.

② **Lightweight**
(25-28 stitches per 4"/10cm)
Includes sport yarn, sock yarn, UK 4-ply, and lightweight DK yarns. The range of needle sizes is 3-6 (3.25-4mm).

③ **Medium Weight**
(21-24 stitches per 4"/10cm)
Includes DK and worsted, the most commonly used knitting yarns. The range of needle sizes is 6-9 (4-5.5mm).

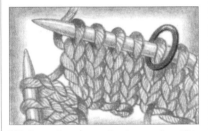

Work until you reach the marker. This completes the first round. Slip the marker to the right needle and work the next round.

④ **Medium-heavy Weight**
(17-20 stitches per 4"/10cm)
Also called heavy worsted or Aran. The range of needle sizes is 8-10 (5-6mm).

⑤ **Bulky Weight**
(13-16 stitches per 4"/10cm)
*Also called chunky. Includes heavier Icelandic yarns.
The range of needle sizes is 10-11 (6-8mm).*

holding the iron 2"/5cm above the knitting. Do not press or it will flatten stitches.

FINISHING

The pieces in this book use a variety of finishing techniques from cutting steek stitches in the Man's Fair Isle Vest (page 24), to joining shoulders with the three-needle bind-off method (page 14), used in the Checked Pullover (page 59). Directions for embroidery stitches are on page 14, duplicate stitch on page 17

⑥ **Extra-bulky Weight**
(9-12 stitches per 4"/10cm)
The heaviest yarns available. The range of needle sizes is 11 and up (8mm and up).

SEWING

When using a very bulky or highly textured yarn, it is sometimes easier to seam pieces together with a finer, flat yarn. Just be sure that your sewing yarn closely matches the original yarn used in your project in color and washability.

CARE

Refer to the yarn label for the recommended cleaning method. Many of the projects in the book can be either washed by hand or in the machine on a gentle or wool cycle, in lukewarm water with a mild detergent. Do not agitate or soak for more than 10 minutes. Rinse gently with tepid water, then fold in a towel and gently press the water out. Lay flat to dry away from excess heat and light. Check the yarn label for any specific care instructions such as dry cleaning or tumble drying.

LAZY DAISY STITCH

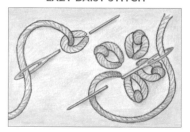

FRENCH KNOT

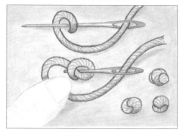

THREE-NEEDLE BIND-OFF

1 With RS placed together, hold pieces on two parallel needles. Insert a third needle knitwise into the first stitch of each needle, and wrap the yarn around the needle as if to knit.

2 Knit these two stitches together, and slip them off the needles. *Knit the next two stitches together in the same manner.

3 Slip the first stitch on the third needle over the second stitch and off the needle. Repeat from the * in Step 2 across the row until all stitches have been bound off.

There are different ways to make a yarn over. Which method to use depends on where you are in the stitch pattern. If you do not make the yarn over in the right way, you may lose it on the following row, or make a yarn over that is too big. Here are the different variations:

Between two knit stitches: Bring the yarn from the back of the work to the front between the two needles. Knit the next stitch, bringing the yarn to the back over the right-hand needle, as shown.

Between a knit and a purl stitch: Bring the yarn from the back to the front between the two needles. Then bring it to the back over the right-hand needle and back to the front again, as shown. Purl the next stitch.

Between a purl and a knit stitch: Leave the yarn at the front of the work. Knit the next stitch, bringing the yarn to the back over the right-hand needle, as shown.

Between two purl stitches: Leave the yarn at the front of the work. Bring the yarn to the back over the right-hand needle and to the front again, as shown. Purl the next stitch.

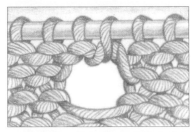

Multiple yarn overs (two or more): Wrap the yarn around the needle, as when working a single yarn over, then continue wrapping the yarn around the needle as many times as indicated. Work the next stitch of the left-hand needle. On the following row, work stitches into the extra yarn overs as described in the pattern. The illustration at right depicts a finished yarn over on the purl side.

CHAIN

1 *Pass the yarn over the hook and catch it with the hook.*

2 *Draw the yarn through the loop on the hook.*

3 *Repeat steps 1 and 2 to make a chain.*

SINGLE CROCHET

1 *Insert the hook through top two loops of a stitch. Pass the yarn over the hook and draw up a loop—two loops on hook.*

2 *Pass the yarn over the hook and draw through both loops on hook.*

3 *Continue in the same way, inserting the hook into each stitch.*

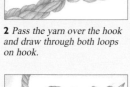

HALF-DOUBLE CROCHET

1 *Pass the yarn over the hook. Insert the hook through the top two loops of a stitch.*

2 *Pass the yarn over the hook and draw up a loop—three loops on hook. Pass the yarn over the hook.*

3 *Draw through all three loops on hook.*

DOUBLE CROCHET

1 *Pass the yarn over the hook. Insert the hook through the top two loops of a stitch.*

2 *Pass the yarn over the hook and draw up a loop—three loops on hook.*

3 *Pass the yarn over the hook and draw it through the first two loops on the hook, pass the yarn over the hook and draw through the remaining two loops. Continue in the same way, inserting the hook into each stitch.*

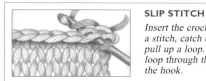

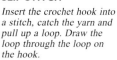

SLIP STITCH

Insert the crochet hook into a stitch, catch the yarn and pull up a loop. Draw the loop through the loop on the hook.

Illustrations: Joni Coniglio

TO BEGIN SEAMING

If you have left a long tail from your cast-on row, you can use this strand to begin sewing. To make a neat join at the lower edge with no gap, use the technique shown here. Thread the strand into a yarn needle. With the right sides of both pieces facing you, insert the yarn needle from back to front into the corner stitch of the piece without the tail. Making a figure eight with the yarn, insert the needle from back to front into the stitch with the cast-on tail. Tighten to close the gap.

INVISIBLE SEAMING: STOCKINETTE ST

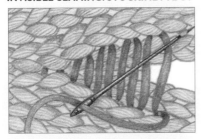

To make an invisible side seam in a garment worked in stockinette stitch, insert the yarn needle under the horizontal bar between the first and second stitches. Insert the needle into the corresponding bar on the other piece. Pull the yarn gently until the sides meet. Continue alternating from side to side.

DUPLICATE STITCH

Duplicate stitch covers a knit stitch. Bring the needle up below the stitch to be worked. Insert the needle under both loops one row above and pull it through. Insert it back into the stitch below and through the center of the next stitch in one motion, as shown.

KNITTING TERMS AND ABBREVIATIONS

approx approximately

beg begin(ning)

bind off Used to finish an edge and keep stitches from unraveling. Lift the first stitch over the second, the second over the third, etc. (UK: cast off)

cast on A foundation row of stitches placed on the needle in order to begin knitting.

CC contrast color

ch chain(s)

cm centimeter(s)

cont continue(ing)

dc double crochet (UK: tr-treble)

dec decrease(ing)–Reduce the stitches in a row (knit 2 together).

dpn double-pointed needle(s)

foll follow(s)(ing)

g gram(s)

garter stitch Knit every row. Circular knitting: knit one round, then purl one round.

hdc half double crochet (UK: htr-half treble)

inc increase(ing)–Add stitches in a row (knit into the front and back of a stitch).

k knit

k2tog knit 2 stitches together

LH left-hand

lp(s) loop(s)

m meter(s)

MI make one stitch–With the needle tip, lift the strand between last stitch worked and next stitch on the left-hand needle and knit into the back of it. One knit stitch has been added.

MI-p make one purl stitch–With the needle tip, lift the strand between last stitch worked and next stitch on the left-hand needle and purl into the back of it. One purl stitch has been added.

MC main color

mm millimeter(s)

no stitch On some charts, "no stitch" is indicated with shaded spaces where stitches have been decreased or not yet made. In such cases, work the stitches of the chart, skipping over the "no stitch" spaces.

oz ounce(s)

p purl

p2tog purl 2 stitches together

pat(s) pattern

pick up and knit (purl) Knit (or purl) into the loops along an edge.

pm place markers–Place or attach a loop of contrast yarn or purchased stitch marker as indicated.

psso pass slip stitch(es) over

rem remain(s)(ing)

rep repeat

rev St st reverse Stockinette stitch–Purl right-side rows, knit wrong-side rows. Circular knitting: purl all rounds. (UK: reverse stocking stitch)

rnd(s) round(s)

RH right-hand

RS right side(s)

sc single crochet (UK: dc–double crochet)

sk skip

SKP Slip 1, knit 1, pass slip stitch over knit 1.

SK2P Slip 1, knit 2 together, pass slip stitch over the knit 2 together.

sl slip–An unworked stitch made by passing a stitch from the left-hand to the right-hand needle as if to purl.

sl st slip stitch (UK: single crochet)

ssk slip, slip, knit–Slip next 2 stitches knitwise, one at a time, to right-hand needle. Insert tip of left-hand needle into fronts of these stitches from left to right. Knit them together. One stitch has been decreased.

sssk Slip next 3 sts knitwise, one at a time, to right-hand needle. Insert tip of left-hand needle into fronts of these stitches from left to right. Knit them together. Two stitches have been decreased.

st(s) stitch(es)

St st Stockinette stitch–Knit right-side rows, purl wrong-side rows. Circular knitting: knit all rounds. (UK: stocking stitch)

tbl through back of loop

tog together

WS wrong side(s)

wyib with yarn in back

wyif with yarn in front

work even Continue in pattern without increasing or decreasing. (UK: work straight)

yd yard(s)

yo yarn over–Make a new stitch by wrapping the yarn over the right-hand needle. (UK: yfwd, yon, yrn)

* = repeat directions following * as many times as indicated.

[ ] = Repeat directions inside brackets as many times as indicated.

PATTERN STITCH VEST
To dye for

For Experienced Knitters

Handpainted yarns steal the show in this design by Margaret Stove—guaranteed to add pizzazz to any man's wardrobe. A solid-color stockinette back balances the brightly-colored pattern stitches on the front, while a shaped lower edge, garter-stitch trim, and smart buttons add polish.

SIZES
Instructions are written for Man's size Small. Changes for sizes Medium and Large are in parentheses.

KNITTED MEASUREMENTS
■ Chest 40 (44, 48)"/101.5 (111.5, 122)cm
■ Length 24 (25, 26)"/61 (63.5, 66)cm

MATERIALS
■ 5 (6, 7) 1¾oz/50g skeins (each approx 88yds/80m) of Brown Sheep *Handpaint Originals* (mohair/wool④) each in #HP80 green (MC) and #HP75 multi (CC)
■ One pair size 8 (5mm) needles *or size to obtain gauge*
■ Size 7 (4.5mm) circular needle, 29"/74cm long
■ Five ¾"/20mm buttons

GAUGE
18 sts and 23 rows to 4"/10cm over St st using larger needles.
Take time to check gauge.

Note
Shoulders are shaped using short rows.

DAISY STITCH
(multiple of 4 sts plus 3)
Row 1 (WS) K3, *work daisy st (p3tog but do not drop sts from needle, yo wrapping yarn completely around needle, p same 3 sts tog again, drop sts from needle—one daisy st made), k1; rep from * to end.
Rows 2 and 4 Knit.
Row 3 *K1, work daisy st; rep from * end, k3.
Rep rows 1-4 for daisy st.

WRAP & TURN (W&T)
RS rows Sl the next st purlwise to RH needle, wyif, sl the same st back to LH needle, turn work.
WS rows Sl the next st purlwise to RH needle, wyib, sl the same st back to LH needle, turn work.

BACK
With larger needles and MC, cast on 91 (100, 108) sts. Work in St st until piece measures 14 (14½, 15)"/35.5 (37, 38)cm from beg.
Armhole shaping
Bind off 2 sts at beg of next 2 rows, then dec 1 st each side every other row 4 times—79 (88, 96). Work even until armhole measures 9 (9½, 10)"/23 (24, 25.5)cm.
Shoulder shaping
K to last 9 (10, 11) sts. W&T.

Sl 1, p to last 9 (10, 11) sts, W&T.
Sl 1, k to last 18 (20, 22) sts, W&T.
Sl 1, p to last 18 (20, 22) sts, W&T.
Sl 1 k to last 27 (30, 33) sts, W&T.
Sl 1 p to last 27 (30, 33) sts, W&T.
Sl 1 k to end.
Bind off, working the wrap tog with the sl st.

LEFT FRONT
With larger needles and CC, cast on 31 (35, 39) sts. K 1 row.
Beg lower edge shaping
Row 1 (WS) Cast on 4 sts, k3, *work daisy st, k1; rep from * to end.
Row 2 and all RS rows Knit.
Row 3 Cast on 4 sts, k4, *k1, work daisy st; rep from *, end k3.
Row 5 Cast on 3 sts, k2, *work daisy st, k1; rep from * to end.
Row 7 Cast on 2 sts, k1, *k1, work daisy st; rep from *, end k3.
Row 9 Cast on 1 st, k1, *work daisy st, k1; rep from * to end.
Row 11 Inc 1 in first st, k1, *k1, work daisy st; rep from *, end k3.
Row 13 Inc 1 in first st, k1, *work daisy st, k1; rep from * to end.
Row 15 Inc 1 in first st, *work daisy st, k1; rep from *, end k2.
Row 17 K4, *work daisy st, k1; rep from * to end.
Row 19 Inc 1 in first st, *k1, work daisy st; rep from *, end k3.
Row 21 K1, *work daisy st, k1; rep from * to end.
Row 23 Inc 1 in first st, k2, *work daisy st,

k1; rep from *, end k2.
Row 25 K2, *work daisy st, k1; rep from * to end.
Row 27 Cast on 1 st, k1, *work daisy st, k1; rep from *, end k2.
Cont in daisy st on 51 (55, 59) sts until piece measures 14 (14½, 15)"/35.5 (37, 38) from beg, end with a WS row.
Neck and armhole shaping
Dec 1 st at armhole edge every other row 4 times, AT SAME TIME, dec 1 st at neck edge every 4th row 17 (18, 19) times—30 (33, 36) sts. Work even until piece measures same as back to shoulder, beg shoulder shaping.
Shoulder shaping
Work to last 10 (11, 12) sts, W&T.
Sl, k to end.
Work to last 20 (22, 24) sts, W&T.
Sl, k to end.
Bind off loosely.

RIGHT FRONT
Work to correspond to left front, reversing all shaping.

FINISHING
Block pieces to measurements. Sew shoulder seams.
Armhole bands
With RS facing, circular needle and MC, pick up and k 81 (86, 90) sts along armhole edge.
Rows 1, 4 and 8 With MC, knit.
Rows 2, 3, 6 and 7 With CC, knit.
Row 5 With MC, purl.

Bind off loosely with MC.

Back edging

With RS facing, circular needle and MC, pick up and k 91 (100, 108) sts along lower edge of back. Work as for armhole band.

Front edging

With RS facing, circular needle and MC, pick up and k 31 (35, 39) sts along lower edge of right front, 11 sts around shaping, 16 sts along front to neck shaping, 53 (56, 60) sts along right neck edge, 25 (28, 30) sts across back neck, 53 (56, 60) sts along left neck edge, 16 sts along left front to shaping, 11 sts around shaping, 31 (35, 39) sts along lower edge of left front— 247 (264, 282) sts.

Work as for armhole band, working rows 2 and 4 as foll:

Row 2 K37 (41, 45), [M1, k5] twice, M1, k to last 47 (51, 55) sts, [M1, k5] twice, M1, k37 (41, 45).

Row 4 K37 (41, 45), inc 1 in next st, [k5, M1] twice, work to V-neck shaping on left front, [k2tog, yo, k7] 5 times (for buttonholes), k to last 47 (51, 55) sts, M1, [k5, M1] twice, k37 (41, 45).

Sew side and armhole band seams. Sew on buttons opposite buttonholes.

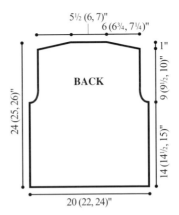

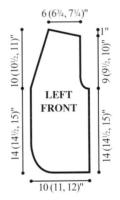

Country gentleman

Inspired by a creek near her home, Diane Zangl's vest design echoes the colors of dark winter clouds, patches of sky, and red willow bushes. Perfect for business or casual wear, it is knit in the round using steeks to create the armholes and neck, and features Fair Isle on the front and checks on the back.

SIZES
Instructions are written for Man's size Small. Changes for sizes Medium and Large are in parentheses.

KNITTED MEASUREMENTS
- Chest 40 (43, 47)"/101.5 (109, 119.5)cm
- Length 26 (26½, 28)"/66 (67.5, 71)cm

MATERIALS
- 4 (4, 5) 1¾oz/50g skeins (each approx 175yds/158m) of Koigu Wool Designs *Premium Merino* (wool②) in #2410 dk blue (MC)
- 2 skeins each in #2130 turquoise (A), #2416 denim (B) and #2390.5 ecru (C)
- 1 skein each in #2239 burgundy (D), #2238 red (E) and #2323 lt blue (F)
- One each sizes 4 and 5 (3.5 and 3.75mm) circular needles, 16"/40cm and 24"/60cm long *or size to obtain gauge*
- Stitch holder and markers

GAUGE
26 sts and 28 rows to 4"/10cm over Fair Isle chart pat using larger needles.
Take time to check gauge.

Notes
1 Piece is worked in the rnd using steek sts. Steek sts are cut later to create openings for the armhole and neck.
2 Steek sts are not included in st counts.
3 Front is worked in Fair Isle pat and back is worked in small check pat.

STITCH GLOSSARY
S2KP
Sl 2 tog knitwise, k1, pass the 2 slipped sts over the knit st.

BODY
With smaller needle and MC, cast on 236 (248, 276) sts. Join, taking care not to twist sts on needle. Mark end of rnd and sl marker every rnd. Work in k2, p2 rib for 2¼ (2¼, 2½)"/6 (6, 6.5)cm. Change to larger needle and k 1 rnd, inc 26 (30, 30) sts evenly spaced—262 (278, 306) sts.
Beg chart
Work Fair Isle chart over 131 (139, 153) sts, beg and end as indicated for chosen size, working 12-st rep 10 (11, 12) times. Work check chart across next 131 (139, 153) sts. Cont as established until piece measures 15 (15, 16)"/38 (38, 40.5)cm from beg.
Armhole shaping
Work 105 (109, 119), bind off next 26 (30, 34) sts (left armhole), work 105 (109, 119) sts, bind off next 26 (30, 34) sts (right armhole), work to end.
Next rnd Cast on 7 steek sts over bound-off sts. Join and cont on all sts (work steek

sts in colorwork pat), and dec 1 st at each armhole edge (inside of steek sts) every other rnd 6 (6, 7) times—186 (194, 210) sts, AT SAME TIME, when armhole measures 1"/2.5cm, beg neck shaping.

Neck shaping

Work 46 (48, 52) sts, place center st on a holder, work to end.

Next rnd Cast on 7 steek sts over center st for neck. Dec 1 st at each neck edge (inside of steek sts) every other rnd 26 (27, 29) times (changing to shorter needle when necessary)—133 (139, 151) sts. Work even until armhole measures 11 (11½, 12)"/28 (29, 30.5)cm.

Bind off 7 steek sts for left armhole, 20 (21, 23) sts for left front shoulder, 7 steek sts for front neck, 20 (21, 23) sts for right front shoulder, 7 steek sts for right armhole, 20 (21, 23) sts for right back shoulder, sl next 53 (55, 59) sts on a holder for back neck, bind off rem 20 (21, 23) sts for left back shoulder.

FINISHING

Block piece to measurements. Cut all steeks. Sew shoulder seams.

Armhole bands

With shorter, smaller needle and MC, beg at underarm, pick up and k 172 (176, 184) sts around armhole edge. Join and work in k2, p2 rib for 1"/2.5cm. Bind off in rib.

Neckband

With longer, smaller needle join MC and work in k2, p2 rib across 53 (55, 59) sts of back neck holder, dec 1 (3, 3) sts evenly spaced, pick up and k 70 (74, 76) sts along left front, pm, k center st from holder, pick up 70 (74, 76) sts along right front—193 (201, 209) sts, pm for end of rnd.

Next (dec) rnd Work in k2, p2 rib to 1 st before center marker, S2KP, rib to end. Rep dec rnd until neckband measures 1"/2.5cm. Bind off in rib.

Turn steeks to inside and sew in place. For more information on steek knitting, see *Vogue Knitting* Fall '89.

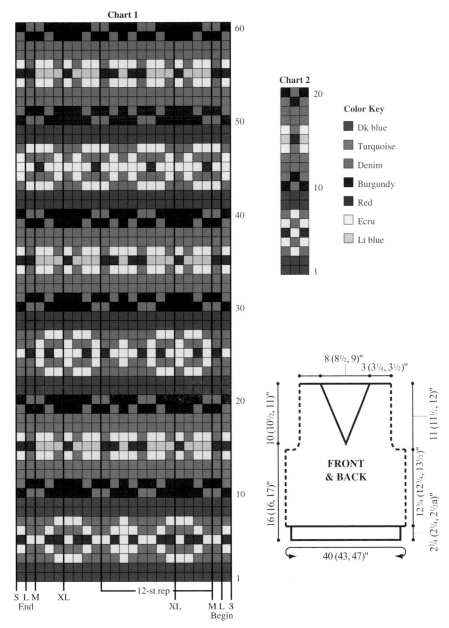

Chart 1

60

50

40

30

20

10

1

S L M   XL   12-st rep   M L S
End   XL   Begin

Chart 2

20

10

1

Color Key

■ Dk blue
■ Turquoise
■ Denim
■ Burgundy
■ Red
□ Ecru
□ Lt blue

8 (8½, 9)"
3 (3¼, 3½)"

10 (10½, 11)"

11 (11½, 12)"

FRONT & BACK

16 (16, 17)"

12¾ (12¾, 13½)"

2¼ (2¼, 2½a)"

40 (43, 47)"

Great Scottie

Sasha Kagan pairs hounds with houndstooth checks in this delightful child's vest. Scotties prance between rows of checks in two sizes, while a touch of red adds a dash of spice to the crisp black-and-white design. A stylish V-neck and twisted-rib trim top it off.

SIZES

Instructions are written for Babies size 12 months. Changes for Child's Size 4/6 are in parentheses.

KNITTED MEASUREMENTS

■ Chest 22½ (30)"/57 (76)cm
■ Length 12½ (14½)"/32 (37)cm

MATERIALS

■ 1 (2) 1¾oz/50g skeins (each approx 187yds/170m) of Rowan Yarns *True 4-Ply Botany* (wool②) each in #546 black (A) and #545 white (B)
■ 1 (2) .88oz/25g skeins (each approx 163 yds/148m) *Rowanspun 4 Ply Tweed* (wool②) each in #704 slate (C) and #710 burgundy (D)
■ One pair each sizes 2 and 4 (2.5 and 3.5mm) needles *or size to obtain gauge*
■ Stitch holders

GAUGE

34 sts and 36 rows to 4"/10cm over chart pat using larger needles.
Take time to check gauge.

Twisted Rib

(even number of sts)
Row 1 *K1 tbl, p1; rep from * to end.
Rep row 1 for twisted rib.

BACK

With smaller needles and A, cast on 96 (128) sts. Work in twisted rib for 1"/2.5cm. Change to larger needles.

Beg chart
Work 32-st rep of chart 3 (4) times, working rows 1-56 once, k 1 row A, then rep rows 41-56 until piece measures 7 (8)"/18 (20.5)cm from beg, end with a WS row.

Armhole shaping
Bind off 5 sts at beg of next 2 rows, then dec 1 st each side every other row 6 (8) times—74 (102) sts. Work even until armhole measures 5 (6)"/12.5 (15)cm, end with a WS row.

Shoulder shaping
Bind off 11 (17) sts at beg of next 4 rows. Place rem 30 (34) sts on a holder for back neck.

FRONT

Work as for back until piece measures measures 7"/18cm from beg, end with a WS row.

Armhole and neck shaping
Bind off 5 sts at beg of next 2 rows.
Next row (RS) K2tog, work 40 (56) sts, place rem sts on a holder.
Working left side of front only, work 1 row even. Cont to shape armhole at beg of RS rows as for back, AT SAME TIME,

dec 1 st at neck edge every other row 13 (15) times—22 (34) sts. Work even until piece measures same as back to shoulder, then shape shoulder as for back.

Join yarn, sl next 2 sts to a holder, then work right side of front to correspond to left side, reversing all shaping.

FINISHING

Block pieces to measurements. Sew right shoulder seam.

Neckband

With RS facing, circular needle and A, beg at left front shoulder, pick up and k 39 (46) sts along left neck edge, pm, k2 sts from holder, pm, pick up and k 39 (46) sts along right neck edge, k 30 (34) sts from back neck holder—110 (128) sts. Work in twisted rib as foll:

Row 1 (WS) Rib to 2 sts before marker, p2tog, sl marker, p2, sl marker, p2tog tbl, rib to end.

Row 2 Rib to 2 sts before marker, SKP, sl marker, k2, sl marker, k2tog, rib to end.

Rep last 2 rows twice more. Change to D and rep row 1 once. Bind off loosely in rib, working tog 2 sts before and after marked center sts.

Armhole bands

Sew left shoulder and neckband seam. With RS facing, smaller needles and A, pick up and k 76 (92) sts evenly around armhole edge. Work in twisted rib for 6 rows, dec 1 st at beg and end of *every* row. Change to D and rib 1 row. Bind off loosely in rib.

Sew side and armhole band seams.

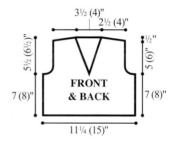

FRONT & BACK

3½ (4)"
2½ (4)"
5½ (6½)"
½"
5 (6)"
7 (8)"
7 (8)"
11¼ (15)"

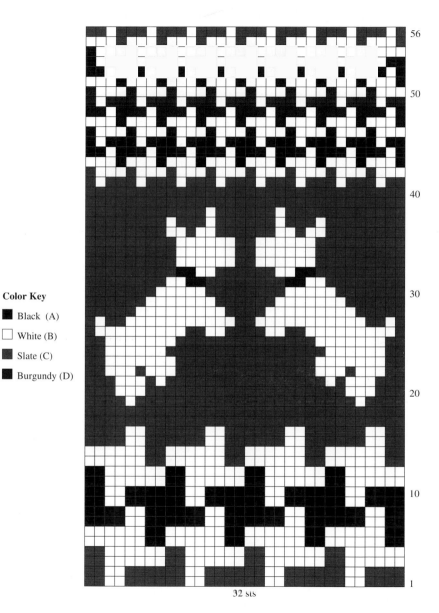

Color Key

■ Black (A)

☐ White (B)

▦ Slate (C)

■ Burgundy (D)

32 sts

Mari Lynn Patrick's tailored vest features interior shaping for a flawless fit. Self-finished edges and a doubled collar and lapels set off the simple styling, while whimsical buttons add pizazz.

SIZES

Instructions are written for Woman's size Small. Changes for sizes Medium and Large are in parentheses.

KNITTED MEASUREMENTS

- Lower edge 39½ (41½, 43)"/100 (105, 109)cm
- Waist 32 (34, 35½)"/81 (86.5, 90)cm
- Bust 35½ (37½, 39½)"/90 (95, 100)cm
- Length 24½ (25, 25½)"/62 (63.5, 65)cm

MATERIALS

- 10 (10, 12) 1¾oz/50g balls (each approx 88yd/80m) of Filatura Di Crosa/Tahki•Stacy Charles, Inc. *Luna* (wool④) in #223 red
- One pair size 9 (5.5mm) needles *or size to obtain gauge*
- Two size 9 (5.5mm) dpn
- Five ⅞"/22mm buttons

GAUGE

17 sts and 23 rows to 4"/10cm over St st using size 9 (5.5mm) needles.
Take time to check gauge.

Note K1 selvage sts at each end of row are not figured into the finished measurements.

BACK

Cast on 86 (90, 94) sts.

Row I (RS) K1 (selvage st), p to last st, k1 (selvage st). Then beg with a p row, work in St st for 3"/7.5cm.

Dec row (RS) K16, pm, k1, sl this st back to LH needle and pull the next 2 sts over this st one at a time (for 2-st right dec), k to last 19 sts, SK2P (for 2-st left dec), pm, k16. Rep dec row (right dec after first marker and left dec before 2nd marker) every 12th row 3 times more—70 (74, 78) sts. Work even for 5 rows. Piece measures 10½"/26.5cm from beg.

Inc row (RS) K1, inc 1 st in next st, k to last 3 sts, inc 1 st in next st, k2. Rep inc row every 10th row 3 times more—78 (82, 86) sts. Work even until piece measures 17"/43cm from beg.

Armhole shaping

Bind off 4 (4, 5) sts at beg of next 2 rows.

Dec row (RS) K3, p1, k2, 2-st right dec, k to last 9 sts, 2-st left dec, k2, p1, k3. Rep dec row every 4th row once, every 6th row twice—54 (58, 60) sts. Work even until armhole measures 6½ (7, 7½)"/16.5 (18, 19)cm.

Neck and shoulder shaping

Bind off 5 (5, 6) sts at beg of next 2 rows, 4 (5, 5) sts at beg of next 4 rows, AT SAME TIME, bind off center 18 sts and working both sides at once, bind off 5 sts from each neck edge once.

LEFT FRONT

Cast on 48 (50, 52) sts.

Row I (RS) K1 (selvage st), purl to end.

Next row (WS) Cast on 5 sts (for front facing), p4, sl 1 (for turning st), p4, k1, p to last st, k1 (selvage st)—53 (55, 57) sts.
Next row (RS) K to last 10 sts, p1, k9. Cont in this way until piece measures 3"/7.5cm from beg.
Dec row (RS) K16, pm, work 2-st right dec, work to end. Rep dec row (dec 2 sts after marker) every 12th row 3 times more—45 (47, 49) sts. Place a yarn marker (for neck) at center front edge on last dec row.

Lapel shaping
Read before beg to knit.
Work even for 5 rows.
Inc row (RS) K1, inc 1 st in next st, work to end. Rep inc row every 10th row 3 times more, AT SAME TIME when 11 (13, 15) rows OR 2 (2¼, 2½)"/5 (6, 6.5)cm from yarn marker at neck, beg lapel shaping as foll: K to last 12 sts, k2tog, p1, inc 1 st in next st, k to last st, inc 1 st in last st. (Note that the k2tog before the p1 st is a single right dec and the inc 1 after the p1 st plus the inc 1 st at the end of row is a double inc.) Rep single right dec every alternate 2nd and 4th rows a total of 12 times more, AT SAME TIME, rep double inc every 2nd row 18 times more, AND, work armhole shaping at side edge when same length as back. There are 62 (64, 65) sts after all shaping and lapel increases. Place a yarn marker at lapel edge. Work even for 2½"/6.5cm or 14 rows from yarn marker.

End lapel
Next row (WS) P10, turn, leaving rem sts unworked.
Next row (RS) Bind off 3 sts, k to end. P1 row. Rep last 2 rows once.
Next row Bind off 2 sts, k to end. P 1 row. Bind off 2 sts (this is the inner lapel facing). Return to lapel sts and purl with dpn, p until there are 13 sts, then turn needles with right side facing tog and p 13 sts from dpn tog with next 13 sts on working needles while binding off (for finishing inside top lapel seam). Then, turn lapel seam to right side and cont on rem 26 (28, 29) sts shaping neck by binding off 3 sts from neck edge every other row twice, 2 sts twice, 1 st 3 times. When same length as back, shape shoulder as on back. Place markers for 5 buttons along center front band, the first one on 9th row from lower edge and the others evenly spaced to the top one at beg of lapel shaping.

RIGHT FRONT

Work to correspond to left front, reversing all shaping (working left decs and left single dec as ssk instead of k2tog at lapel), placement of front facing and working double buttonholes opposite markers as foll: **Buttonhole row (RS)** K1, k2tog, yo, k3, yo, k2tog, k to end.

FINISHING

Block pieces to measurements turning front facing at foldline and pressing top lapel seam flat. Sew shoulder and side seams. Split yarn in half and tack front facing and lapel facing in place inside of the k1 st on WS. Block flat.

Collar

Leaving first 12 sts of right lapel and last 12 sts of left lapel free, pick up and k 77 sts evenly around neck edge from RS of garment.

Row 1 (WS) Inc 1 st, (for selvage st), p to last st, inc 1 st (for selvage st). Work in St st for 3"/7.5cm or 17 rows. P next row on RS for turning ridge. Work in St st for 16 rows more. Bind off. Fold collar to inside and sew invisibly over seam line. (Collar should show no seam on RS or WS). Sew on buttons. Fold back collar and lapels and steam lightly.

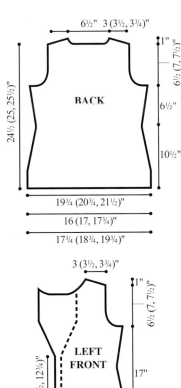

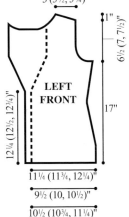

BI-COLOR VEST
Opposites attract

High-contrast stripes and blocks pack a lively punch in Irina Poludnenko's garter-stitch vest. Alternating points form a clever button closure, and a two-button flap accents the back.

SIZES
Instructions are written for Woman's size Small. Changes for sizes Medium and Large are in parentheses.

KNITTED MEASUREMENTS
- Bust 38 (43, 48)"/96.5 (109, 122)cm
- Length 21 (23, 24)"/53.5 (58.5, 61)cm

MATERIALS
- 5 (5, 6) 1¾oz/50g skeins (each approx 85yds/78m) of Berroco, Inc. *Cotton Twist* (cotton/viscose③) each in #8366 pink (A) and #8388 purple (B)
- One pair size 8 (5mm) needles *or size to obtain gauge*
- Six ⅝"/15mm buttons
- Stitch holders

GAUGE
20 sts and 34 rows to 4"/10cm over garter st using size 8 (5mm) needles.
Take time to check gauge.

BACK
Left back
**With A, cast on 48 (54, 60) sts. K 28 rows. Change to B. Inc 1 st at beg of every other row 7 times—55 (61, 67) sts.

Next (buttonhole) row (RS) K1, k2tog, bind off 2 sts, k to end. Cast on 2 sts over the bound-off sts on next row. Then dec 1 st at beg of every other row 6 times more—48 (54, 60) sts**. Place sts on a holder.

Right back
**With B, cast on 48 (54, 60) sts. Inc 1 st at end of every other row 7 times—55 (61, 67) sts.

Next (buttonhole) row(RS) K to last 6 sts, bind off 2 sts, k to end. Cast on 2 sts over the bound-off sts on next row. Then dec 1 st at end of every other row 7 times—48 (54, 60) sts. Change to A and k 28 rows.** With B, k48 (54, 60), with A, work across 48 (54, 60) sts from left back holder—96 (108, 120) sts. Work in garter st in colors as established until piece measures 12½ (14, 14½)"/32 (35.5, 37)cm from beg.

Armhole shaping
Cont in colors as established and bind off 8 sts at beg of next 2 rows. Dec 1 st each side every other row 5 (5, 4) times 70 (82, 96) sts. Work even until armhole measures 7½ (8, 8½)"/19 (20.5, 21.5)cm.

Shoulder shaping
Bind off 4 (5, 6) sts at beg of next 8 rows. Bind off rem 38 (42, 48) sts for back neck.

LEFT FRONT
Work from ** to ** twice as for left back (4 color panels).

Neck and armhole shaping
Dec 1 st at neck edge every other row 2 (0,

3) times, every 4th row 17 (21, 21) times, AT SAME TIME, when piece measures 12½ (14, 14½)"/32 (35.5, 37)cm from beg, shape armhole at beg of RS rows as for back. Work even until piece measures same as back to shoulder, then shape shoulder as for back.

RIGHT FRONT

Work from ** to ** twice as for right back (4 color panels). Change to A. Work as for left front, reversing all shaping.

FINISHING

Block pieces to measurements. Sew shoulder seams. Sew side seams. Sew buttons on opposite buttonholes.

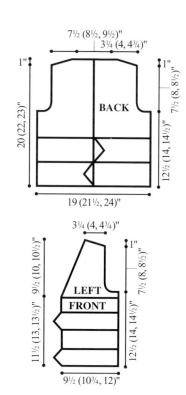

TEXTURED TOGGLE VEST
Beginner basics

A chunky, nubby thick-and-thin yarn offers tons of texture and instant gratification to novice knitters with this design by Bonnie Franz. Rows of basic knit and purl create the ridged pattern, and toggle buttons offer a simple closure.

SIZES
Instructions are written for Woman's size Small. Changes for sizes Medium and Large are in parentheses.

KNITTED MEASUREMENTS
■ Bust 40 (46, 50)"/101.5 (117, 127)cm
■ Length 21 (22, 24)"/53.5 (56, 61)cm

MATERIALS
■ 5 (6, 7) 3½oz/100g skeins (each approx 81yds/73m) of Bouton d'Or/ Anny Blatt *Flocon* (wool/polyamide ⑥) in #017 gold
■ Small amount of plain yarn for seaming
■ One pair size 13 (9mm) needles *or size to obtain gauge*
■ Size 13 (9mm) circular needles, 16"/40cm and 32"/80cm long
■ Five 2"/50mm toggles

GAUGE
9 sts and 14 rows to 4"/10cm over pat st using size 13 (9mm) needles.
Take time to check gauge.

Pattern Stitch
Row 1 (WS) Knit.
Row 2 Purl.
Rows 3-12 Work in St st.
Rep rows 1-12 for pat st.

BACK
Cast on 45 (52, 56) sts. Work in pat st until piece measures 12 (12½, 13½)"/30.5 (32, 34.5)cm.
Armhole shaping
Bind off 2 sts at beg of next 2 rows—41 (48, 52) sts. Work even until armhole measures 9 (9½, 10½)"/23 (24, 26.5)cm. Bind off.

LEFT FRONT
Cast on 22 (26, 28) sts. Work as for back until piece measures same as back to armhole.
Armhole and neck shaping
Work as for back, working armhole shaping at beg of RS rows, AT SAME TIME, dec 1 st at neck edge every other row 0 (1, 0) time, then every 4th row 7 (7, 8) times. Cont in pat until piece measures same as back to shoulder. Bind off rem 13 (16, 18) sts for shoulder.

RIGHT FRONT
Work to correspond to left front, reversing all shaping.

FINISHING

Block pieces to measurements. With plain yarn, sew shoulder and side seams.

Front edging

Place markers on right front edge for 5 buttonholes, the first one 1 st from lower edge, the last one just below first neck dec, and three others spaced evenly between. With RS facing and longer circular needle, pick up and k 118 (136, 154) sts along right front, back neck and left front edges. K 1 row.

Next (buttonhole) row (RS) K1, *k2tog, yo, work to next marker; rep from * 4 times more, k to end. K 1 row. Bind off.

Armhole bands

With RS facing and shorter circular needle, pick up and k 48 (50, 58) sts around armhole edge. Join and k 1 row, p 1 row. Bind off.

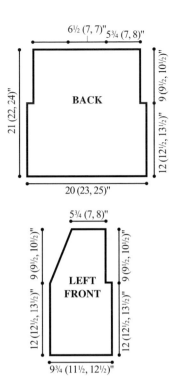

This smart little vest is a stand out thanks to snappy colors brightening the traditional geometric Fair Isle patterning. Bright red seed-stitch edgings add a simple finish. Designed by Jean Guirguis.

SIZES

Instructions are written for Child's size 12 months. Changes for sizes 2 and 3 are in parentheses.

KNITTED MEASUREMENTS

▪ Chest 24 (26, 28)"/61 (66, 71)cm
▪ Length 10 (11, 12)"/25.5 (28, 30.5)

MATERIALS

▪ 1 (2, 2) 1¾oz/50g balls (each approx 193 yds/175m) of Dale of Norway *Baby Ull* (wool②) in #4018 red (A)
▪ 1 ball each in #6714 aqua (B), #2317 yellow (C), #7436 green (D), #8523 lt green (E) and #5726 blue (F)
▪ One pair each sizes 1 and 2 (2.25 and 2.5mm) needles *or size to obtain gauge*
▪ Size 1 (2.25mm) circular needle, 16"/40cm long
▪ Stitch holders

GAUGE

28 sts and 36 rows to 4"/10cm over St st using larger needles.
Take time to check gauge.
Note Carry yarn not in use loosely across back of work.

Seed Stitch

(even number of sts)
Row 1 *K1, p1; rep from * to end.
Row 2 K the purl sts and p the knit sts.
Rep rows 1 and 2 for seed st.

BACK

With smaller needles and A, cast on 80 (86, 94) sts. Work in seed st for ¾"/2cm, end with a RS row. P 1 row, inc 5 sts evenly spaced—85 (91, 99) sts.
Beg Fair Isle chart
Beg and end as indicated, work foll chart until piece measures 6 (5½, 6)"/15 (14, 15)cm from beg.
Armhole shaping
Bind off 5 sts at beg of next 2 rows, 3 sts at beg of next 2 rows, dec 1 st each side every other row 3 times—63 (69, 77) sts. Work even until armhole measures 4 (5½, 6)"/10 (14, 15)cm. Place sts on holder.

FRONT

Work as for back until armhole measures 2 (3½, 4)"/5 (9, 10)cm.
Neck shaping
Next row (RS) K24 (27, 31), sl next 15 sts to holder, join a 2nd ball of yarn and work to end. Working both sides at once, bind off 2 sts from each neck edge 4 times. Sl rem 16 (19, 23) sts each side to holder for shoulders.

FINISHING

Block pieces to measurements. Join shoulders using 3-needle bind-off. Sew side seams.

Neckband

With RS facing, circular needle and A, pick up and k 88 around neck edge. Join and work 6 rnds in seed st. Bind off.

Armhole band

With RS facing, circular needle and A, pick up and k 68 (94, 104) along armhole edge. Join and work 6 rnds in seed st. Bind off.

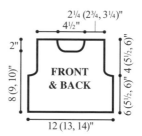

2¼ (2¾, 3¼)"
4½"
2"
8 (9, 10)"
FRONT & BACK
6 (5½, 6)" 4 (5½, 6)"
12 (13, 14)"

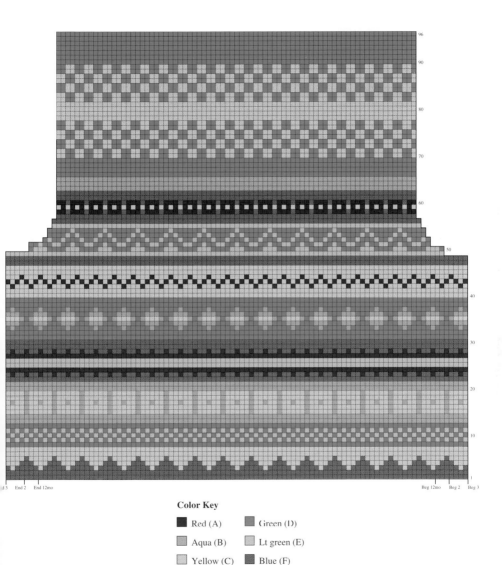

Color Key

■ Red (A)	■ Green (D)
■ Aqua (B)	■ Lt green (E)
■ Yellow (C)	■ Blue (F)

HOODED VEST

Under cover

For Intermediate Knitters

Heather Lodinsky's space-dyed vest blends the best features of a favorite sweatshirt: a cozy hood, roomy set-in pockets, and a zippered front. A luscious rayon/silk tape yarn and a woven-cable pattern on the yoke add individual style.

SIZES

Instructions are written for Woman's size Small. Changes for sizes Medium and Large are in parentheses.

KNITTED MEASUREMENTS
- Bust 36½ (41, 46.5)"/92.5 (104, 118)cm
- Length 18 (20, 22)"/45.5 (51, 56)cm

MATERIALS
- 4 (5, 6) 4oz/125g skeins (each approx 280yds/252m) of Cherry Tree Hill Yarns *Silky Pastels* (rayon/silk②) in blue/green multi
- Size 7 (4.5mm) circular needle, 32"/80cm long
- Cable needle
- Stitch holders and markers
- 16 (18, 20)"/40 (46, 51)cm separating zipper

GAUGE

19 sts and 32 rows to 4"/10cm over garter st using size 7 (4.5mm) needles.
Take time to check gauge.

Woven Cable Pattern
(multiple of 6 sts plus 2)
Row 1 (RS) Knit.

Row 2 Knit.
Row 3 K1, *k1 wrapping yarn twice around needle; rep from *, end k1.
Row 4 K1, *dropping extra lps, sl 3 sts to cn and hold to *back*, k3, k3 from cn; rep from * end k1.
Rows 5 and 6 Knit.
Row 7 K4, *k1 wrapping yarn twice around needle; rep from * to last 4 sts, k4.
Row 8 K4, *dropping extra lps, sl 3 sts to cn and hold to *front*, k3, k3 from cn; rep from * to last 4 sts, k4.
Rep rows 1-8 for woven cable pat.

BACK
Cast on 88 (100, 112) sts. Work in garter st for 9 (10, 12)"/23 25.5, 30.5)cm, end with a WS row.
Armhole shaping
Bind off 5 sts at beg of next 2 rows, 3 sts at beg of next 2 rows, dec 1 st each side every other row twice—68 (80, 92) sts.
Beg woven cable pat
Work in woven cable pat until armhole measures 9 (10, 10)"/23 (25.5, 25.5)cm, end with row 4 or 8. Bind off.

LEFT POCKET
Cast on 42 (48, 54) sts. Work in garter st for 2 (2½, 3)"/5 (6.5, 7.5)cm, end with a WS row.
Next row (RS) Bind off 4 sts, k to end. K 1 row. Dec 1 st at beg of each RS row 26 times—12 (18, 24) sts. Place sts on a holder.

LEFT FRONT
Cast on 42 (48, 54) sts. Work in garter st

until piece measures 5¼ (7½, 9¼)"/13.5 (19, 23.5)cm, end with a WS row.

Pocket joining

Next row (RS) K30, *work first st of pocket tog with first st of front; rep from * across all sts from holder.

Cont in garter st until piece measures same length as back to armhole. Shape armhole at beg of RS rows as for back.

Beg woven cable pat

Work in woven cable pat until armhole measures 7 (8, 8)"/18 (20.5, 20.5)cm, end with RS row.

Neck shaping

Next row (WS) Bind off 14 sts (neck edge), work to end. Cont to bind off at neck edge, 2 sts once, 1 st twice—14 (20, 26) sts. Work even until same length as back to shoulder. Bind off.

RIGHT POCKET AND FRONT

Work to correspond to left pocket and front, reversing all shaping.

FINISHING

Block pieces to measurements. Sew shoulder seams.

Hood

With RS facing, beg at left front, pick up and k 80 sts evenly around neck. Work in garter st until piece measures 9½"/24cm, end with a RS row.

Next row (WS) K40, pm, k40.

Next (dec) row K to 2 sts before marker, ssk, sl marker, k2tog, k to end. Cont in garter st and rep dec row every 6th row 5 times more—68 sts. Bind off. With WS tog, fold hood in half and sew seam.

Armhole bands

With RS facing, pick up and k 121 (134, 134) sts evenly around armhole edge. K 6 rows. Bind off.

Pocket trim

With RS facing, beg after bound-off sts and pick up and k 24 (36, 48) sts along shaped edge of pocket. Work in garter st, inc 1 st each side every other row 3 times. Bind off.

Front and neck band

Sew pocket edges and trim to fronts. With RS facing, pick up and k 76 (86, 95) sts along right front, 134 sts around hood, 76 (86, 95) sts along left front—286 (306, 324) sts. K 6 rows. Bind off.

Sew side seams and armhole bands. Sew in zipper.

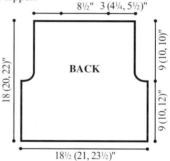

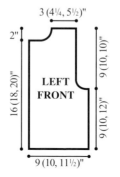

BOY'S CABLE VEST
Racing stripes

From the first day of school to the last, this cool vest wins the vote for best dressed. Designed by **Norah Gaughan**, it showcases panels of ribbing, horseshoe cables, and basketweave with bright stripes highlighting the lower edge and chest.

SIZES

Instructions are written for Child's size 4. Changes for sizes 6 and 8 are in parentheses.

KNITTED MEASUREMENTS

- Chest 25 (28, 30)"/63.5 (71, 76)cm
- Length 16 (17, 18)"/40.5 (43, 46)cm

MATERIALS

- 2 (3, 3) 3½oz/100g skeins (each approx 220yds/200m) of Reynolds/JCA *Signature* (acrylic/wool⑤) in #42 olive (MC)
- 1 skein in #22 pumpkin (CC)
- One pair each sizes 4 and 6 (3.5 and 4mm) needles *or size to obtain gauge*
- Size 4 (3.5m) circular needle, 16"/40cm long
- Cable needle

GAUGE

21 sts and 30 rows to 4"/10cm over rib and cable pat (slightly stretched) using larger needles.
Take time to check gauge.

STITCH GLOSSARY

6-st RC

Sl 3 sts to cn and hold to *back*, k3, k3 from cn.

6-st LC

Sl 3 sts to cn and hold to *front*, k3, k3 from cn.

BACK

With smaller needles and CC, cast on 66 (74, 78) sts. Work in k2, p2 rib as foll: 1 row CC, 2 rows MC, 2 rows CC, then cont in rib with MC only until piece measures 2"/5cm from beg, end with a RS row. Change to larger needles.

Next row (WS) P16 (20, 22), M1, p6, M1, p22, M1, p6, M1, p16 (20, 22)—70 (78, 82) sts.

Beg cable and rib pat

Sizes 4 and 8 Work chart 1 over 12 (18) sts, 16 sts of cable chart, 14 sts in rib as established, 16 sts of cable chart, work chart 2 over last 12 (18) sts.

Size 6 Beg with st 3, work chart 1 over first 16 sts, 16 sts of cable chart, 14 sts in rib as established, 16 sts of cable chart, work chart 2 over last 16 sts, end with st 4. Cont in pats as established until piece measures 6¼ (6¾, 7¼)"/16 (17, 18.5)cm from beg. Cont in cable and rib pat and work 4 rows CC, 4 rows MC, 8 rows CC, 4 rows MC, 4 rows CC, then cont with MC to end of piece. Work even until piece measures 9½ (10, 10½)"/24 (25.5, 26.5cm from beg.

Armhole shaping

Bind off 4 sts at beg of next 2 rows, 3 sts at beg of next 2 rows, 2 sts at beg of next

2 rows, then dec 1 st each side every other row 3 times—46 (54, 58) sts. Work even until armhole measures 5½ (6, 6½)"/14 (15, 16.5)cm.

Shoulder shaping
Bind off 5 (6, 7) sts at beg of next 4 (6, 4) rows, 4 (0, 6) sts at beg of next 2 rows. Place rem 18 sts on holder for back neck.

Work as for back until armhole measures 1"/2.5cm.

Neck shaping
Next row (RS) Work 23 (27, 29) sts, join 2nd ball of yarn and work to end. Working both sides at once, dec 1 st at each neck edge every other row 5 (3, 1) times, every 4th row 4 (6, 8) times. Work even until piece measures same as back to shoulder. Shape shoulders as for back.

FINISHING
Block pieces to measurements. Sew shoulder seams.

Armhole bands
With RS facing, smaller needles and MC, pick up and k 86 (90, 94) evenly along armhole edge. Work in k2, p2 rib for 1"/2.5cm. Bind off in rib.
Sew side and armhole band seams.

Neckband
With RS facing, circular needle and MC, work in rib as established across 18 sts from back neck holder, pick up and k 32 (36, 40) sts along left front, pm, 2 sts at center front, pm, 32 (36, 40) sts along right front—84 (92, 100) sts. Join and

work in rnds of k2, p2 rib as foll: rib to 2 sts before marker, k2tog, k2, ssk, rib to end. Work 1 rnd even. Rep these 2 rnds 3 times more. Bind off in rib

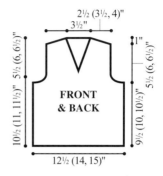

FRONT & BACK

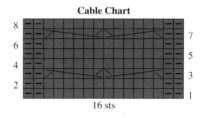

Cable Chart

16 sts

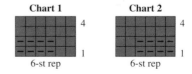

Chart 1

6-st rep

Chart 2

6-st rep

Stitch Key

K on RS, p on WS

P on RS, k on WS

6-st RC

6-st LC

DIAMOND LACE VEST

Watercolors

Argyle patterning accented with lace stitches, and the subtle contrast of soft colors add a delicate touch to this elegant vest designed by Gayle Bunn, making it a chic topper for everything from a T-shirt to a silk blouse.

SIZES

Instructions are written for Woman's size Small. Changes for sizes Medium and Large are in parentheses.

KNITTED MEASUREMENTS

■ Bust (buttoned) 38 (39½, 42¼)"/96.5 (100, 107)cm
■ Length 23 (24½, 24)"/58.5 (60, 61)cm

MATERIALS

■ 4 (4, 5) 1¾oz/50g skeins (each approx 128yds/117m) of Patons® *Country Garden DK* (wool③) in #34 blue (MC)
■ 3 (3, 4) skeins in #30 green (A)
■ One each sizes 3 and 6 (3 and 4mm) circular needles, 40"/100cm long *or size to obtain gauge*
■ Five ⅝"/15mm buttons

GAUGE

22 sts and 30 rows to 4"/10cm over chart pat using larger needles.
Take time to check gauge.

Note Vest is worked in one piece to the underarm.

BODY

With smaller needle and MC, cast on 199 (213, 227) sts. Join, taking care not to twist sts on needle. Place marker for end of rnd and sl marker every rnd.
Next rnd (RS) K2, *p1, k1; rep from *, end k1. Cont in k1, p1 rib for 5 rows more.

Beg chart pat

Change to larger needle. **Next rnd** Beg with st 1, work through 14-st rep, then work 14-st rep 13 (14, 15) times more, work last 2 sts of chart. Cont in pat as established, rep rows 3 to 26, until piece measures 15½"/39.5cm from beg.

Divide for armholes

Next row (RS) Work 41 (44, 45) sts and sl to a holder (right front), bind off 16 (18, 22) sts, work 85 (89, 93) sts and sl to a holder (back), bind off 16 (18, 22) sts, work to end (left front).

LEFT FRONT

Work 1 row even.

Armhole and neck shaping

Next row (RS) Dec 1 st at beg of row (armhole edge) and dec 1 st at end of row (neck edge). Work 1 row even. Rep last 2 rows 8 (9, 10) times more—23 (24, 23) sts. Dec 1 st at neck edge only every other row 4 (4, 1) times, then every 4th row 4 (4, 6) times—15 (16, 16) sts. Work even until armhole measures 7½ (8, 8½)"/19 (20.5, 21.5)cm, end with a WS row. Bind off.

RIGHT FRONT

Join yarn and work to correspond to left front, reversing all shaping.

BACK

Join yarn and work 1 row even.

Armhole shaping

Dec 1 st each side every other row 9 (10, 11) times—67 (69, 71) sts. Work even until piece measures same as left front to shoulder. Bind off.

FINISHING

Block to measurements. Sew shoulder seams.

Button band

With MC and smaller needle, cast on 9 sts.

Row 1 (RS) K2, [p1, k1] 3 times, k1.

Row 2 [K1, p1] 4 times, k1.

Rep these 2 rows until piece, when slightly stretched, fits along left front edge to beg of neck shaping. Sew in place. Place markers for buttons as foll: the first one $\frac{1}{2}$"/1.5cm below neck shaping, the last one $\frac{1}{2}$"/1.5cm above lower edge and 3 others spaced evenly between.

Cont in rib along left front, back neck and right front to neck shaping, sewing in place every few inches.

Buttonhole band

Work buttonhole opposite markers as foll: work to marker, bind off 2 sts. Cast on 2 sts over bound-off sts on next row. When band fits to lower edge of right front, bind off. Sew on buttons at markers.

Armhole bands

Work as for button band, sewing to armhole edge every few inches. Sew seam.

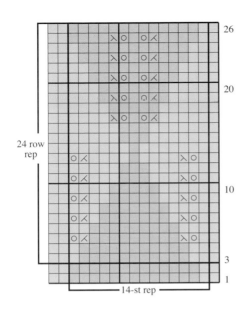

Color Key

■ Blue (MC), K on RS, p on WS

■ Green (A), K on RS, p on WS

⊼ K2tog

⊻ Ssk

○ Yo

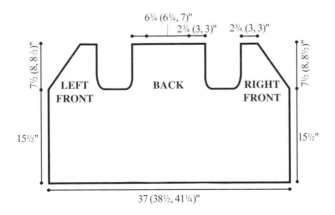

FOURTH OF JULY VEST
Stars and stripes

Every child will shine in Betsy Westman's star-studded cotton topper. Intarsia stars emblazon a red-hot background, while the striped ribbed edging salutes the look.

SIZES

Instructions are written for Child's size 4. Changes for sizes 6 and 8 are in parentheses.

KNITTED MEASUREMENTS

- Chest (buttoned) 32¼ (36½, 39)"/82 (92.5, 99)cm
- Length 15 (17, 18)"/38 (43, 46)cm

MATERIALS

- 5 (5, 6) 1¾oz/50g balls (each approx 110yds/100m) of Trendsetter *Elba* (cotton③) in #516 red (MC)
- 2 (2, 3) balls in #937 white (CC)
- One pair size 4 (3.5mm) needles *or size to obtain gauge*
- Six ½"/13mm buttons
- Bobbins

GAUGE

24 sts and 28 rows to 4"/10cm over St st, using size 4 (3.5mm) needles.
Take time to check gauge.

Notes

1 When changing colors, twist yarns on WS to prevent holes.
2 Use bobbins for each star and carry MC loosely across back of work.

RIB PATTERN

(multiple of 4 sts plus 2)
Row 1 (RS) K2 MC, *p2 CC, k2 MC; rep from * to end.
Row 2 P2 MC, *k2 CC, p2 MC, rep from * to end.
Rep rows 1 and 2 for rib pat.

BACK

Cast on 98 (106, 114) sts. Work in rib pat for 2 (2, 2½)"/5 (5, 6.5)cm.

Beg chart pat

Beg and end as indicated for chosen size, rep rows 1-12 until piece measures 8½ (10, 10½)"/21.5 (25.5, 26.5)cm from beg, end with a WS row.

Armhole shaping

Bind off 3 sts at beg of next 2 rows, dec 1 st each side every other row 3 times—86 (94, 102) sts. Work even until armhole measures 6½ (7, 7½)"/16.5 (18, 19)cm, end with a WS row.

Neck shaping

Next row (RS) Work 24 (26, 30) sts, join 2nd ball of yarn and bind off center 38 (42, 42) sts, work to end. Working both sides at once, work 1 row even. Bind off rem 24 (26, 30) sts each side for shoulder.

LEFT FRONT

Cast on 46 (54, 58) sts. Work as for back until piece measures 8½ (10, 10½)"/21.5 (25.5, 26.5)cm.

Neck and armhole shaping

Next row (RS) Bind off 3 sts (armhole edge), work to last 2 sts, dec 1 st (neck edge). Cont to dec 1 st at armhole edge every other row 3 times and dec 1 st at neck edge every other row 15 (21, 21) times more—24 (26, 30) sts. Work even until piece measures same as back to shoulder. Bind off.

RIGHT FRONT

Work to correspond to left front, reversing all shaping and chart placement.

FINISHING

Block pieces to measurements. Sew shoulder seams.

Armhole band

With RS facing and MC, pick up and k 80 (84, 88) sts evenly along armhole edge. Work 4 rows in rib pat. Bind off with MC.

Neckband

With RS facing and MC, pick up and k 198 (218, 234) sts evenly along right front, back neck and left front. Work 3 rows in rib pat. Place markers for buttons on left front as foll: the first one at V-neck shaping, the last one ¾"/2cm from lower edge and the other 4 spaced evenly between.

Next (buttonhole) row *Rib to opposite marker, bind off 1 st; rep from * 5 times more, rib to end. Cast on 1 st over bound-off st on next row. Rib 1 row even. Bind off with MC. Sew side and armhole band seams. Sew on buttons.

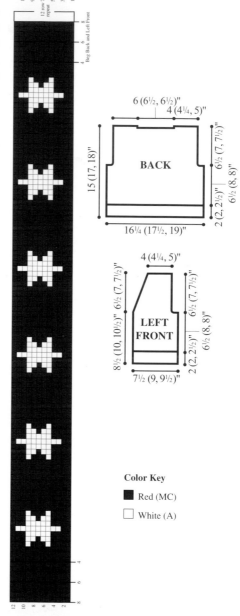

6 (6½, 6½)"
4 (4¼, 5)"

BACK

15 (17, 18)"

6½ (7, 7½)"
6½ (8, 8)"
2 (2, 2½)"

16¼ (17½, 19)"

4 (4¼, 5)"

6½ (7, 7½)"

LEFT FRONT

8½ (10, 10½)" 6½ (7, 7½)"
6½ (7, 7½)"
6½ (8, 8)"
2 (2, 2½)"

7½ (9, 9½)"

Color Key

■ Red (MC)

□ White (A)

CHECKED PULLOVER
Fifties flair

Snappy gingham-style checks lend timeless appeal to Jean Schafer-Albers' pullover vest. Slip stitch creates the check pattern and ribbing trims the armholes and lower edges. A square neckline and chic linen-stitch belt completes the look.

SIZES

Instructions are written for Woman's size Small. Changes for sizes Medium and Large are in parentheses.

KNITTED MEASUREMENTS

- Bust 38 (40½, 43)"/96.5 (103, 109)cm
- Length 24 (24½, 25)"/61 (62, 63.5)cm

MATERIALS

- 4 (4, 5) 1¾oz/50g balls (each approx 112yds/90m) of Lane Borgosesia *Maratona*® (wool⑤) each in #20266 grey (A) and #95013 black (C)
- 3 (3, 4) balls in #1205 ecru
- One pair each sizes 5 and 8 (3.75 and 5mm) needles *or size to obtain gauge*
- Size 8 (5mm) circular needle, 16"/40cm long
- Size G/6 (4mm) crochet hook
- Stitch holders
- 1"/2.5cm belt buckle by Jan Tay #B618 in silver

GAUGE

24 sts and 30 rows to 4"/10cm over check pat using larger needles.
Take time to check gauge.

Check Pattern

(multiple of 4 sts plus 2)
Note Slip all sts purlwise.
Row 1 (WS) With A, purl.
Row 2 With B, k1, sl 1, *k2, sl 2; rep from *, end last rep sl 1, k1.
Row 3 With B, p1, sl 1, *p2, sl 2; rep from *, end last rep sl 1, p1.
Row 4 With A, knit.
Row 5 With C, p2, *sl 2, p2; rep from * to end.
Row 6 With C, k2, *sl 2, k2; rep from * to end.
Rep rows 1-6 for check pat.

Linen Stitch

(even number of sts)
Note Slip all sts purlwise.
Row 1 (RS) *K1, sl 1 wyif, bring yarn to back between needles; rep from *, end k2.
Row 2 *P1, sl 1 wyib, bring yarn to back between needles; rep from *, end p2.
Rep rows 1 and 2 for linen st.

BACK

With larger needles and C, cast on 114 (122, 130) sts. Work in k1, p1 rib for 1"/2.5cm, end with a RS row. Work in check pat until piece measures 15½"/39.5cm from beg.

Armhole shaping

Bind off 9 sts at beg of next 2 rows, 2 sts at beg of next 4 rows, dec 1 st each side every other row 3 (4, 5) times—82 (88, 94) sts. Work even until armhole measures 7½ (8, 8½)"/19 (20.5, 21.5)cm, end with a WS row.

Neck shaping

Next row (RS) Work 24 (26, 28) sts, join 2nd ball of yarn and bind off center 34 (36, 38) sts, work to end. Work both sides at once until armhole measures 8½ (9, 9½)"/21.5 (23, 24)cm. Place rem 24 (26, 28) sts each side on holders for shoulders.

FRONT

Work as for back until armhole measures 5½ (6, 6½)"/14 (15.5, 16.5)cm, end with a WS row.

Neck shaping

Next row (RS) Work 24 (26, 28) sts, join 2nd ball of yarn and bind off center 34 (36, 38) sts, work to end. Work both sides at once until piece measures same as back to shoulder. Place rem 24 (26, 28) sts each side on holders for shoulders.

FINISHING

Block pieces to measurements. Join shoulders using 3-needle bind-off. Sew side seams.

Neck edging

With RS facing, crochet hook and C, work an edge of sc evenly around neck.

Armhole bands

With RS facing, circular needle and C, pick up and k 110 (116, 122) sts evenly around armhole edge. Join and work in rnds of k1, p1 rib for 1"/2.5cm. Bind off in rib.

BELT

With smaller needles and C, cast on 8 sts. Work in linen st until piece measures desired length plus 1"/2.5cm. Bind off. Sew belt to buckle.

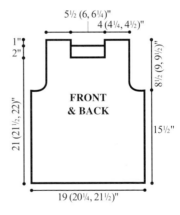

CABLE VEST
Celtic charm

For Experienced Knitters

Long and slim, this stunning vest by Fiona Ellis will become an enduring classic. Celtic-style knots embellish the lower edge, then taper into long, classic cables that create a stream-lined effect. Fine black edgings add a dash of sophistication.

SIZES
Instructions are written for Woman's size Small. Changes for sizes Medium and Large are in parentheses.

KNITTED MEASUREMENTS
- Bust 35 (40, 44)"/89 (101.5, 112)cm
- Length 24 (24½, 25)"/61 (62, 63.5)cm

MATERIALS
- 10 (11, 13) 1¾oz/50g balls (each approx 65yds/59m) of Classic Elite Yarns *Bazic Wool* (wool④) in #2857 blue (MC)
- 1 ball in #2913 black (CC)
- One pair size 9 (5.5mm) needles *or size to obtain gauge*
- Cable needle
- Size H/8 (5mm) crochet hook
- Two ¾"/20mm buttons

GAUGE
21 sts and 23 rows to 4"/10cm over cable chart using size 9 (5.5mm) needles.
Take time to check gauge.

STITCH GLOSSARY
3-st RPC
Sl 1 st to cn and hold to *back*, k2, p1 from cn.

3-st LPC
Sl 2 sts to cn and hold to *front*, p1, k2 from cn.

4-st RC
Sl 2 sts to cn and hold to *back*, k2, k2 from cn.

4-st LC
Sl 2 sts to cn and hold to *front*, k2, k2 from cn.

4-st RPC
Sl 2 sts to cn and hold to *back*, k2, p2 from cn.

4-st LPC
Sl 2 sts to cn and hold to *front*, p2, k2 from cn.

BACK
With CC, cast on 92 (106, 116) sts. Work in k1, p1 rib for 1 row. Change to MC and p 1 row.

Beg chart pat
Work row 1 of chart as foll:

Size Small Work sts 9 to 28 four times, 9 to 20 once.

Size Medium Work sts 9 to 20, 1 to 28, 9 to 20, p2, 9 to 20, 1 to 28, 9 to 20.

Size Large P5, *work sts 9 to 20, 1 to 28, 9 to 20, p2; rep from *, end p3.

Cont as established through row 4. Then rep rows 1-4 until piece measures 15"/38cm from beg.

Armhole shaping
Bind off 3 sts at beg of next 2 rows, then dec 1 st each side *every* row 10 (12, 12) times— 66 (76, 86) sts. Work even until armhole measures 8 (8½, 9)"/20.5 (21.5, 23)cm.

Neck and shoulder shaping
Next row (RS) Work 18 (20, 22) sts, join 2nd ball of yarn, bind off center 30 (36, 42) sts, work to end. Dec 1 st at each neck edge *every* row twice, AT SAME TIME, bind off 8 (9, 10) sts from each shoulder edge twice.

LEFT FRONT

With CC, cast on 46 (52, 57) sts. Work in k1, p1 rib for 1 row. Change to MC and p 1 row.

Beg chart pat

Work row 1 of chart as foll:

Size Small P6, work sts 1 to 28, 9 to 20.

Size Medium Work sts 9 to 20, 1 to 28, 9 to 20.

Size Large P5, work sts 9 to 20, 1 to 28, 9 to 20.

Cont as established through row 58. Then rep rows 1-4 only until piece measures 15"/38cm from beg, end with a WS row.

Armhole and neck shaping

Shape armhole as for back at beg of RS rows, AT SAME TIME, dec 1 st at neck edge every other row 11 (14, 18) times, every 4th row 6 (5, 4) times—16 (18, 20) sts. When piece measures same as back to shoulder, shape shoulders as for back.

RIGHT FRONT

Work to correspond to left front, reversing all shaping and chart placement.

FINISHING

Block pieces to measurements. Sew shoulder seams.

Armhole edging

With crochet hook and CC, sc evenly around armhole edges.

Front edging

With crochet hook and CC, beg at lower right front edge, sc along right front to neck shaping, ch 1, turn. **Next row** Work 1 sc, *ch 3, skip 1 st, sc in next 3 sts; rep from * once, ch 1, turn. **Next row** *Sc in next 2 sts, 5 sc into ch; rep from * once, then cont to work a row of sc around right neck edge, back neck and left front.

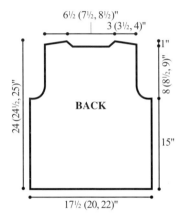

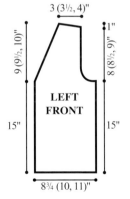

Stitch Key

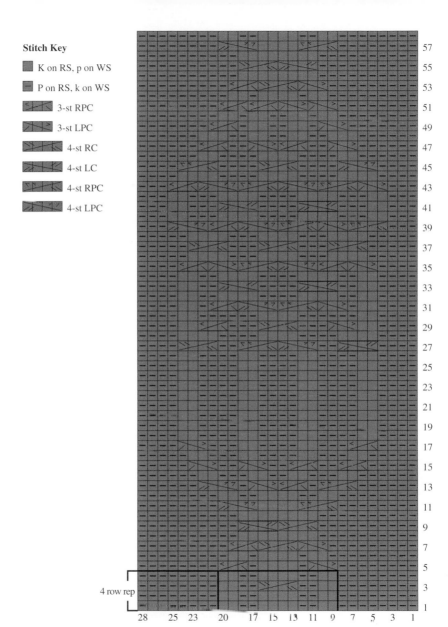

- K on RS, p on WS
- P on RS, k on WS
- 3-st RPC
- 3-st LPC
- 4-st RC
- 4-st LC
- 4-st RPC
- 4-st LPC

4 row rep

BELTED TABARD
Green piece

Nancy Marchant's intricately patterned tabard is simpler to knit than it looks: it is worked in one piece, from back to front. Slip stitches create the color pattern and side vents add flair. A two-color ribbed belt makes a fashionable finish.

SIZES

Instructions are written for Woman's size Small. Changes for sizes Medium and Large are in parentheses.

KNITTED MEASUREMENTS

- Bust 39½ (45, 50)"/100.5 (114.5, 127)cm
- Length 28½ (29½, 30½)"/72.5 (75, 77.5)cm

MATERIALS

- 1 5oz/250g skeins (each approx 525 yds/472m) of Woolpak Yarns NZ/ Baabajoe's Wool Co. *8 Ply* (wool ④) each in mallard (A), #30 green (B), #12 dk green (C), #19 nutmeg (D) and #10 black (E)
- One pair size 7 (4.5mm) needles *or size to obtain gauge*
- Two size 7 (4.5mm) dpn
- Size E/4 (3.5mm) crochet hook
- Stitch holder

GAUGE

18 sts and 33 rows to 4"/10cm over pat st, using size 7 (4.5mm) needles.
Take time to check gauge.

Notes

1 Vest is worked in one piece from back to lower edge of fronts.
2 Carry yarn loosely along side edge.

Pattern Stitch

(multiple of 6 sts plus 5)
Set up row 1 (RS) With A, k2, *k1 wrapping yarn twice around needle (k1w), k5; rep from *, end k1w, k2.
Change to B.
Row 1 (WS) K2, *sl 1 wyif (dropping the 2nd wrap), k5; rep from *, end sl 1 wyif, k2.
Row 2 K2, *sl 1 wyib, k2, k1w, k2; rep from *, end sl 1 wyib, k2.
Change to C.
Row 3 *K5, sl 1 wyif (dropping the 2nd wrap); rep from *, end k5.
Row 4 K2, *k1w, k2, sl 1 wyib, k2; rep from *, end k1w, k2.
With D, rep rows 1 and 2.
With E, rep rows 3 and 4.
With A, rep rows 1 and 2.
With B, rep rows 3 and 4.
With C, rep rows 1 and 2.
With D, rep rows 3 and 4.
With E, rep rows 1 and 2.
With A, rep rows 3 and 4.
Rep these 20 rows for pat st.

BACK

Cast on 89 (101, 113) sts. Work in pat st until piece measures 28 (29, 30)"/71 (73.5, 76)cm from beg.

DIVIDE FOR FRONTS

Next row (RS) Pm. Work 33 (39, 45) sts and place rem sts on a holder for left front. Work 1 row even.

RIGHT FRONT
Neck shaping

Dec 1 st at neck edge on next row, then every other row 3 times more—29 (35, 41) sts. Work even until piece measures 29 (30, 31)"/73.5 (76, 78.5)cm from marker.

LEFT FRONT

Join yarn, bind off 23 sts for neck, work to end. Then cont as for right front, reversing all shaping.

FINISHING

Block to measurements.
With crochet hook and E, work an edge of sc around all edges.

BELT

With dpn and E, cast on 14 sts.
Row 1 With C, *k1, p1; rep from * to end.
Row 2 With E, slide sts to other end of needle, *k1, p1; rep from * to end.
Row 3 With C, turn *k1, p1; rep from * to end.
Rep rows 2 and 3 until piece measures 50"/127cm (or desired length), end with row 3. Bind off with E.

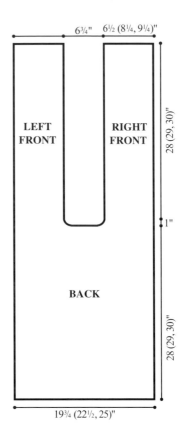

6¾"   6½ (8¼, 9¼)"

LEFT FRONT   RIGHT FRONT

28 (29, 30)"

1"

BACK

28 (29, 30)"

19¾ (22½, 25)"

DOUBLE-ZIPPERED VEST
Outer space

A basic vest takes on new dimensions when knit in a rich variegated yarn and finished with a folded collar and hem that reveal reverse-stockinette texture. Designed by Nancy Marchant, this sleeveless jacket sports a casual zippered closure.

SIZES

Instructions are written for Woman's size Small. Changes for sizes Medium and Large are in parentheses.

KNITTED MEASUREMENTS

■ Bust 40 (44, 48)"/101.5 (111.5, 122)cm
■ Length 23"/58.5cm

MATERIALS

■ 19 (20, 23) 1¾oz/50g skeins (each approx 55yds/50m) of Naturally/S. R. Kertzer *Colourworks* (wool④) in #993 blue multi
■ One pair each sizes 8 and 10 (5 and 6mm) needles *or size to obtain gauge*
■ Size G/6 (4mm) crochet hook
■ 24"/61cm separating zipper

GAUGE

14 sts and 21 rows to 4"/10cm over St st using larger needles.
Take time to check gauge.

Note Vary skeins of multi-colored yarn throughout to ensure uniform appearance.

BACK

With smaller needles, cast on 68 (74, 82) sts. Work 9 rows in St st, then work 10 rows in rev St st, inc 2 sts evenly spaced on last row—70 (76, 84) sts. Change to larger needles and work in St st until piece measures 16½ (16, 15)"/42 (40.5, 38)cm from beg.

Armhole shaping

Bind off 4 sts at beg of next 2 rows, dec 1 st each side every other row 3 times—56 (62, 70) sts. Work even until armhole measures 7½ (8, 9)"/19 (20.5, 23)cm.

Shoulder shaping

Bind off 5 (6, 7) sts at beg of next 4 (6, 4) rows, 6 (0, 8) sts at beg of next 2 (0, 2) rows. Bind off rem 24 (26, 26) sts for back neck.

LEFT FRONT

With smaller needles, cast on 33 (36, 42) sts. Work as for back, working armhole shaping at beg of RS rows, until armhole measures 6 (6½, 7½)"/15.5 (16.5, 19)cm, end with a RS row.

Neck and shoulder shaping

Next row (WS) Bind off 6 (7, 8) sts, work to end. Cont to bind off at neck edge 3 (3, 4) sts once, 2 sts once, 1 st once—16 (18, 22) sts. When piece measures same as back to shoulder, shape shoulder as for back.

RIGHT FRONT

Work to correspond to left front, reversing all shaping.

FINISHING

Block pieces to measurements. Sew shoulder and side seams.

Crochet edgings

With crochet hook, work a rnd of sc around armhole edges and along front edges.

Neckband

With RS facing and smaller needles, pick up and k 21 (22, 24) sts along right neck edge, 24 (26, 26) sts across back neck, 21 (22, 24) sts along left neck edge—66 (70, 74) sts. Work 8 rows in rev St st, then work 8 rows St st. Bind off.

Fold neckband in half to inside and sew in place.

Fold up hem and sew in place.

Sew in zipper to fronts.

Zipper placket

On WS, pick up and k 3 sts from hem on left front. Work in St st until piece measures same length as front to neckband. Graft sts to neckband hem. Sew placket to zipper and to sweater. Rep for right front.

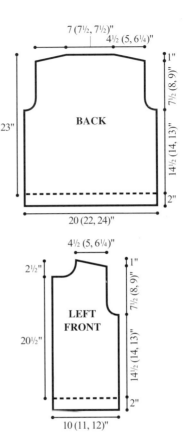

Weekends call for quiet comfort, and Anita Tosten's easygoing vest is the perfect choice. Wide stripes of alternating stockinette and garter are topped with a lattice of long lazy-daisy stitches, while garter-stitch stripes finish the edges.

KNITTED MEASUREMENTS

- Bust 34 (37½, 44½)"/86.5 (95, 113)cm
- Length 19½ (19½, 21½)"/49.5 (49.5, 54.5)cm

MATERIALS

- 2 (2, 3) 1¾oz/50g skeins (each approx 97yds/90m) of Wool in the Woods *Chaps* (wool/alpaca④) each in grey (A) and blue (B)
- One pair size 8 (5mm) needles *or size to obtain gauge*
- Size 8 (5mm) circular needles, 16"/40cm and 29"/74cm long
- Stitch holders
- 8 (8, 9) ¾"/20mm buttons

GAUGE

18 sts and 28 rows to 4"/10cm over pat st using size 8 (5mm) needles.
Take time to check gauge.

Notes

1 Vest is worked in one piece to the underarm.
2 Vary skeins of hand-dyed yarns throughout to ensure uniform appearance.

PATTERN STITCH

(multiple of 16 sts plus 8)
Rows 1, 3, 4, 7 and 9 (RS) With B, knit.
Rows 2, 4, 6, 8 and 10 With B, p8, *k8, p8; rep from * to end.
Rows 11, 13, 15, 17 and 19 With A, knit.
Rows 12, 14, 16, 18 and 20 With A, k8, *p8, k8; rep from * to end.
Rep rows 1-20 for pat st.

BODY

With longer circular needle and A, cast on 152 (168, 200) sts. K 1 row on WS. With B, work in garter st for 2 rows. With A, work in garter st for 2 rows. Then work in pat st until piece measures approx 10 (10, 11)"/25.5 (25.5, 28)cm from beg, end with pat row 10 (10, 20).

Divide for armholes

Work 38 (42, 50) sts and place on a holder (right front), bind off 4 sts, work 68 (76, 92) sts and place on a holder (back), bind off 4 sts, work to end (left front).

LEFT FRONT

Work 1 row even.

Armhole and neck shaping

Cont to bind off at armhole edge, 2 sts once, then dec 1 st at armhole edge every other row 7 times, AT SAME TIME, dec 1 st at neck edge every other row 5 (5, 6) times, every 4th row 11 (13, 14) times— 13 (15, 21) sts. Place shoulder sts on holder.

RIGHT FRONT

Join yarn and work to correspond to left front, reversing all shaping.

BACK

Join yarn and work 1 row even.

Armhole shaping

Cont to bind off from each armhole edge, 2 sts once, then dec 1 st each side every other row 7 times—50 (58, 74) sts. Work even until armhole measures 9 (9, 10)"/23 (23, 25.5)cm.

Neck shaping

Next row (RS) Work 15 (17, 23) sts, place next 20 (24, 28) sts on a holder for back neck, join 2nd ball of yarn, work to end. Working both sides at once, bind off from each neck edge 2 sts once. Work even until piece measures 19½ (19½, 21½)"/49.5 (49.5, 54.5cm from beg. Place rem 13 (15, 21) sts each side on holders for shoulders.

FINISHING

Block to measurements. Using 3-needle bind-off method, bind off shoulder seams tog.

Armhole band

With RS facing, shorter circular needle and A, pick up and k 85 (85, 87) sts around armhole edge. Join and p 1 rnd. With B, k 1 rnd, p 1 rnd. With A, k 1 rnd, p 1 rnd. Bind off loosely with A.

Front bands

With RS facing, longer circular needle and A, pick up and k 38 (38, 43) sts along right front to beg of neck shaping, 45 (45, 50) sts along right neck edge, work across 20 (24, 28) sts from back neck holder, 45 (45, 50) sts along left neck edge to beg of neck shaping, 38 (38, 43) sts along left front—186 (190, 214) sts. K 1 row.

Next (buttonhole) row (RS) With B, k2, yo, k2tog, k1, yo, k2tog, *k3, yo, k2tog; rep from * 5 (5, 6) times more, k to end. K 1 row. With A, k 2 rows. Bind off loosely with A. Sew on buttons opposite buttonholes.

Embroidery

Using lazy daisy st and contrasting color, embroider an "X" in each square of St st, see diagram.

EMBROIDERY DIAGRAM

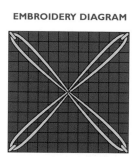

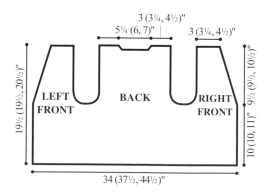

3 (3¼, 4½)"
5¼ (6, 7)"
3 (3¼, 4½)"

19½ (19½, 20½)"

9½ (9½, 10½)"

LEFT FRONT   BACK   RIGHT FRONT

10 (10, 11)"

34 (37½, 44½)"

KANGAROO POUCH VEST

Little boy blue

Nothing gives baby a hop up in the world like this comfy kangaroo-pocket vest designed by Veronica Manno. A neat V-neck offers easy access, and a ribbed edging adds a handsome finish.

SIZES

Instructions are written for Baby's size 6 months. Changes for sizes 12 and 24 months are in parentheses.

KNITTED MEASUREMENTS

- Chest 22 (24, 26)"/56 (61, 66)cm
- Length 10 (11, 13)"/25.5 (28, 33)cm

MATERIALS

- 2 (3, 4) 3½oz/100g skeins (each approx 97yds/90m) of Jaeger Handknits *Baby Merino* (wool③) in #207 lt blue
- One pair size 6 (4mm) needles *or size to obtain gauge*
- Stitch holder

GAUGE

24 sts and 32 rows to 4"/10cm over St st using size 6 (4mm) needles.
Take time to check gauge.

BACK

Cast on 65 (73, 79) sts. Work in k1, p1 rib for 4 rows. Work in St st until piece measures 5½ (6, 7½)"/14 (15.5, 19)cm from beg.

Armhole shaping

Bind off 3 sts at beg of next 2 rows, 2 sts at beg of next 2 rows, dec 1 st each side *every* row 3 (4, 4) times—49 (55, 61) sts.

Work even until armhole measures 4½ (5, 5½)"/11.5 (13, 14)cm. Bind off all sts.

FRONT

Work as for back until armhole measures 1"/2.5cm, end with a WS row.

Neck shaping

Next row (RS) K to center st, sl center st to a holder, join 2nd ball of yarn, work to end. Working both sides at once, dec 1 st at each neck edge every other row 10 (11, 13) times. Work even until piece measures same as back to shoulder. Bind off rem 14 (16, 17) sts each side for shoulders.

POCKET

Cast on 48 (54, 60) sts. Work in St st for 4 rows. Then dec 1 st each side every other row 3 (2, 0) times, every 4th row 3 (4, 6) times—36 (42, 48) sts. Work even until piece measures 4 (4½, 5½)"/10 (11.5, 14)cm from beg. Bind off.

With RS facing, pick up and k 29 (33, 39) sts along one side edge of pocket. Work in k1, p1 rib for 4 rows. Bind off in rib. Rep for other side.

FINISHING

Block pieces to measurements. Center pocket on front, above rib and sew in place. Sew left shoulder seam.

Neckband

With RS facing, pick up and k 29 (31, 37) sts along back neck, 26 (30, 34) sts along left front, pm, k 1 st from holder, pm, 26 (30, 34) sts along right neck—82 (92, 106) sts. Work in k1, p1 for 4 rows, dec 1 st each

side of marker *every* row. Bind off in rib.
Sew right shoulder and neckband seam.

Armhole band

With RS facing, pick up and k 61 (67, 73)
sts around armhole edge. Work in k1, p1
for 4 rows. Bind off in rib.
Sew side and armhole band seams.

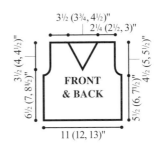

3½ (3¾, 4½)"
2¼ (2½, 3)"
3½ (4, 4½)"
6½ (7, 8½)"
4½ (5, 5½)"
5½ (6, 7½)"

FRONT & BACK

11 (12, 13)"

For Experienced Knitters

From boardroom to golf course, Nancy Marchant's distinguished block vest adds savvy style to today's business-casual dress code. The colorful block pattern on the front blends into one-row striping on the back. Subtle points along the lower front and bi-color ribbed trim lend debonair details.

SIZES

Instructions are written for Man's size Small. Changes for sizes Medium and Large are in parentheses.

KNITTED MEASUREMENTS

■ Chest (buttoned) 40½ (42½, 47)"/103 (108, 119.5)cm
■ Length 20"/51cm

MATERIALS

■ 3 1¾oz/50g skeins (each approx 149 yds/135m) of GGH/Muench Yarns *Classico* (wool/acrylic③) in #9 beige (MC)
■ 1 each in #63 orange (A), #55 green (B), #8 gold (C), #48 rust (D) and #11 dk brown (E)
■ Size 4 (3.5mm) circular needle, 29"/74cm long
■ Four ½"/13mm buttons

GAUGES

■ 21 sts and 30 rows to 4"/10cm over chart pat using size 4 (3.5mm) needles.
■ 22 sts and 28 rows to 4"/10cm over stripe pat, using size 4 (3.5mm) needles. *Take time to check gauge.*

STRIPE PATTERN

Work in St st foll: 1 row A, 1 row B, 1 row C, 1 row D, 1 row E. Slide sts to other end of needle and cont in St st as foll; 1 row MC, 1 row A, 1 row B, 1 row C, 1 row D, 1 row E, slide sts to other end of needle, 1 row MC. Rep these 12 rows for stripe pat.

BACK

With MC, cast on 110 (116, 126) sts. Work in stripe pat until piece measures 9¼"/23.5cm from beg.

Armhole shaping

Bind off 7 sts at beg of next 2 rows, 2 sts at beg of next 4 rows, dec 1 st each side every other row 4 times—80 (86, 96) sts. Work even until armhole measures 10"/25.5cm.

Shoulder shaping

Bind off 7 (8, 10) sts at beg of next 6 (6, 4) rows, 0 (0, 9) sts at beg of next 0 (0, 2) rows. Bind off rem 38 sts for back neck.

LEFT FRONT

With MC, cast on 3 sts. Work foll chart for left front, casting on at lower front where indicated—53 (55, 59) sts. Work even, foll chart for 6"/15cm.

Neck and armhole shaping

Cont to foll chart, dec 1 st at neck edge every 4th row 6 (3, 0) times, every 6th row 11 (13, 15) times, AT SAME TIME, when piece measures same as back to armhole, shape armhole as for back at beg of RS rows. When piece measures same as back to shoulder, shape shoulder as for back.

RIGHT FRONT
Foll chart for right front.

FINISHING
Block pieces to measurements. Sew shoulder seams.
Armhole bands
With RS facing and MC, pick up and k 126 sts along armhole edge.
Row I (WS) *P1, MC, k1 D; rep from * to end.
Row 2 *P1 D, k1 MC; rep from * to end. Rep these 2 rows once more. Bind off in rib with MC.
Neckband
Sew side seams.
With RS facing and MC, beg at lower edge of back, pick up and k 86 (92, 100) sts along back, 32 (34, 36) sts along lower edge of right front, pm, 1 st at center point, pm, 19 sts to front edge, pm, 1 st at center point, pm, 40 sts along front to neck shaping, 84 sts along right neck edge, 38 across back neck, 84 sts along left neck edge to neck shaping, 40 sts along left front, pm, 1 st at center point, pm, 19 sts along lower front edge, pm, 1 st at center point, pm, 32 (34, 36) sts along lower edge of left front—478 (488, 500) sts. Work in rib as for armhole bands, inc 1 st before and after each marker on every row. Place markers for 4 buttons evenly spaced on

right front. Work buttonholes opposite markers on row 3 as foll: Work to marker, yo, k2tog.

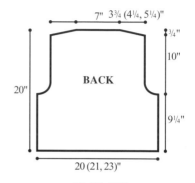

7" 3¾ (4¼, 5¼)"

¾"

10"

BACK

20"

9¼"

20 (21, 23)"

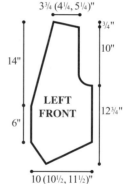

3¾ (4¼, 5¼)"

¾"

10"

14"

LEFT FRONT

12¾"

6"

10 (10½, 11½)"

Color Key

■ Beige (MC)
■ Orange (A)
■ Green (B)
□ Gold (C)
■ Rust (D)
■ Dk Brown (E)

80

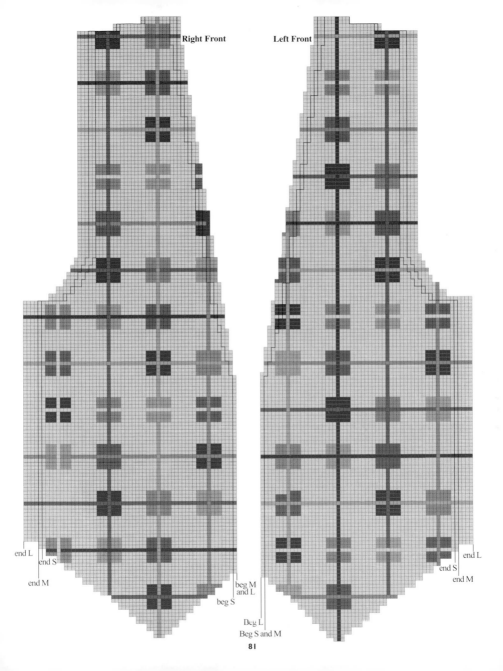

Right Front   **Left Front**

end L

end S

end M

beg M
and L

beg S

Beg L

Beg S and M

end L

end S

end M

MAN'S TWEED VEST
Diamondback

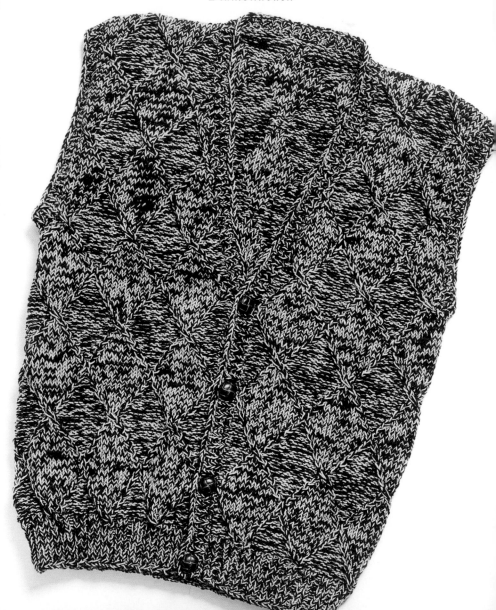

Mary Gildersleeve's marled vest is perfect for cozy fireside evenings. Worked in one piece to the armholes, it features a bold diamond cable pattern, and its tweedy effect is created by one strand each of blue and grey yarn held together.

SIZES

Instructions are written for Man's size Small. Changes for sizes Medium and Large are in parentheses.

KNITTED MEASUREMENTS

- Chest 42 (46½, 54)"/106.5 (118, 137)cm
- Length 26 (28, 29)"/66 (71, 73.5)cm

MATERIALS

- 7 (9, 10) 1¾oz/50g balls (each approx 143yds/130m) of Schoeller Esslinger/Skacel *Merino Soft* (wool③) each in #19 grey (A) and #4 navy (B)
- One each sizes 8 and 10 (5 and 6mm) circular needle needles, 24"/60cm long *or size to obtain gauge*
- Size 8 circular needle, 16"/40cm long
- Cable needle
- Stitch holders
- Four ⅞"/22mm buttons

GAUGE

16 sts and 24 rows to 4"/10cm over chart pat using larger needles and one strand of A and B held tog.
Take time to check gauge.

Notes

1 One strand of A and B are held tog throughout.
2 Vest is worked in one piece to the underarm.
3 First and last st of every row is worked as a rev St st selvage st.

STITCH GLOSSARY

Right Twist (RT)
Pass in front of first st and k 2nd st, then k first st and let both sts fall from needle.

Left Twist (LT)
Pass in back of first st and k 2nd st tbl, then k first st and let both sts fall from needle.

3-st LC
Sl 1 st to cn and hold to *front*, k2, k1 from cn.

BODY

With smaller needles and 1 strand of A and B held tog, cast on 168 (184, 200) sts.
Next row (RS) P1 (selvage st), *k2, p2; rep from *, end k2, p1 (selvage st). Cont in k2, p2 rib as established for 2½"/6.5cm, inc 14 (14, 13) sts evenly spaced on last WS row—182 (198, 213) sts. Change to larger needles.

Beg chart pat
Row 1 (RS) P1 (selvage st), work sts 1 (8, 8) to 15, then work 15-st rep 10 (12, 13) times, then work sts 1 to 15 (8, 8), p1 (selvage st). Cont as established until piece measures 15 (17, 18)"/38 (43, 45.5)cm from beg.

Divide for armholes
Next row (RS) Work 44 (47, 51) sts and sl to a holder (right front), bind off 4 sts, work

86 (96, 103) sts and sl to a holder (back), bind off 4 sts, work to end (left front).

LEFT FRONT
Armhole and neck shaping
Dec 1 st at armhole edge every other row 2 (3, 3) times, AT SAME TIME, dec 1 st at neck edge every other row 16 times. Cont in pat until armhole measures 11"/28cm, end with row 26 (14, 14) of chart. Place rem 26 (28, 32) sts on a holder.

RIGHT FRONT
Join yarn and work to correspond to left front, reversing all shaping.

BACK
Join yarn and work as for left front, omitting neck shaping, until piece measures same length as left front. Place sts on a holder.

FINISHING
Block piece to measurements. Using 3-needle bind-off method, bind off shoulder seams. Sl center 82 (90, 97) sts on holder for back neck.

Armhole bands
With RS facing and 16"/40cm smaller circular needle, beg at shoulder seam, pick up and k 102 sts around armhole edge. Join and work 5 rnds in k1, p1 rib, working k3tog at shoulder on last rnd. Bind off in rib.

Front and neck bands
With RS facing and 24"/60cm long, smaller circular needle, pick up and k 92 sts from right front edge, work across 30 (34, 33) sts of back neck holder, 92 sts from left front edge—214 (218, 217) sts. Work 1 row in k1 p1 rib. Place markers for buttons on right front as foll; the first one at beg of neck shaping, the last one 1"/2.5cm from lower edge and 2 others spaced evenly between.

Next (buttonhole) row (RS) Work buttonholes opposite markers as foll: *k2tog, yo. Work 3 rows more in k1, p1 rib. Bind off in rib.

Sew on buttons at markers.

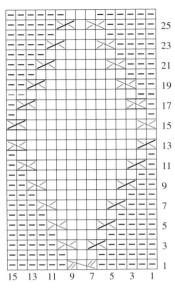

															25
															23
															21
															19
															17
															15
															13
															11
															9
															7
															5
															3
															1

15 13 11 9 7 5 3 1

Stitch Key

☐ K on RS, p on WS

⊟ P on RS, k on WS

⊠ RT

⊠ LT

◨◧ 3-st LC

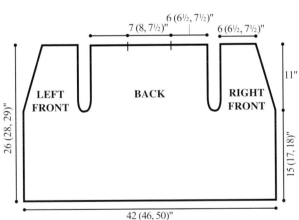

6 (6½, 7½)"

7 (8, 7½)"   6 (6½, 7½)"

LEFT FRONT   BACK   RIGHT FRONT

11"

26 (28, 29)"

15 (17, 18)"

42 (46, 50)"

GIRL'S FAIR ISLE VEST

Savoire "Fair"

Glorious details and spirited colors adorn Mags Kandis's adorable child's vest. Bands of bright Fair Isle decorate the lower half of the front, while lazy daisies bloom across the top.

SIZES

Instructions are written for Child's size 4. Changes for sizes 6 and 8 are in parentheses.

KNITTED MEASUREMENTS

- Chest 27 (29, 31)"/68.5 (73.5, 79)cm
- Length 12 (12, 13)"/30.5 (30.5, 33)cm

MATERIALS

- 2 1¾oz/50g skeins (each approx 84 yds/77m) of Mission Falls/Unique Kolours *1824 Cotton* (cotton④) in #400 fog (A)
- 1 skein each in #103 pebble (B), #405 phlox (C), #402 sea (D), #302 wintergreen (E) and #204 lentil (F)
- One pair each sizes 7 and 8 (4.5 and 5mm) needles *or size to obtain gauge*
- Size F/5 (4mm) crochet hook

GAUGES

- 20 sts and 24 rows to 4"/10cm over Fair Isle chart using larger needles.
- 18 sts and 24 rows to 4"/10cm over St st using larger needles.
Take time to check gauges.

BACK

With smaller needles and B, cast on 60 (64, 70) sts. Work in garter st for 6 rows. inc 8 sts evenly spaced on last row—68 (72, 78) sts. Change to larger needles and D.

Beg Fair Isle chart

Working in St st, beg and end for chosen size and work foll chart. Piece measures approx 7¼"/18.5cm.

Armhole shaping

Bind off 5 sts at beg of next 2 rows, 3 sts at beg of next 2 rows. Change to F and garter st. Bind off 2 sts at beg of next 2 rows, dec 6 sts evenly spaced on last WS row—42 (46, 52) sts.

Yoke

Change to A. Work in St st, dec 1 st each side every other row 2 (3, 4) times—38 (40, 44) sts. Work even until piece measures 11¾ (11¾, 12¾)"/30 (30, 32.5)cm from beg, end with a WS row.

Shoulder shaping

Bind off 4 (5, 5) sts at beg of next 2 rows, 5 (5, 6) sts at beg of next 2 rows. Bind off rem 20 (20, 22) sts for back neck.

LEFT FRONT

With smaller needles and B, cast on 28 (30, 33) sts. Work in garter st for 6 rows. inc 3 sts evenly spaced on last row—31 (33, 36) sts. Cont as for back until piece measures 8¼ (8¼, 9¼)"/21 (21, 23.5)cm, working armhole shaping at beg of RS rows and dec 3 sts (instead of 6) evenly spaced on last row before yoke.

Neck shaping

Cont armhole shaping as for back yoke, dec 1 st at neck edge every other row 7 (7, 8) times—9 (10, 11) sts, AT SAME TIME, when piece measures same as back to shoulder, shape shoulder at beg of RS rows as for back.

Work to correspond to left front, reversing all shaping, and beg and end Fair Isle chart as indicated.

Block pieces to measurements. Sew shoulder seams.

Armhole bands

With RS facing, smaller needles and A, pick up and k 56 (56, 64) sts evenly around armhole. Work in garter st for 3 rows. Bind off.

Sew side seams.

Front edgings

With RS facing, smaller needles and B, pick up and k 37 (37, 41) sts along right front to neck shaping, 18 sts along neck edge, 20 (20, 22) sts across back neck, 18 sts along left neck edge, 37 (37, 41) sts along left front—130 (130, 140) sts. Work in garter st for 3 rows. Bind off.

Crochet edging

With crochet hook and C, work as foll around garter st front edging: sl st into first bound-off st, *ch 4, sl st into next bound-off st; rep from * around. Fasten off.

Embroidery

With C, D, E and F, work Lazy Daisy flowers over yoke on fronts and back.

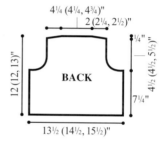

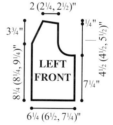

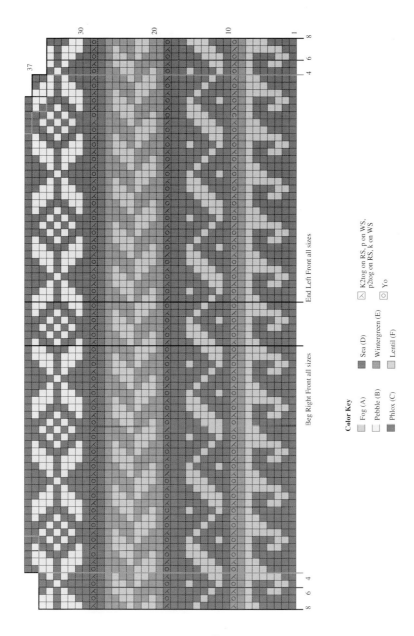

Color Key

Fog (A)
Pebble (B)
Phlox (C)
Sea (D)
Wintergreen (E)
Lentil (F)

K2tog on RS, p on WS, p2tog on RS, k on WS
Yo

Beg Right Front all sizes

End Left Front all sizes

Nicky Epstein's cardigan vest makes spirits bright with festive colors and delightful Christmas motifs. Charming trees, stockings, snowflakes, and more are worked onto colorful squares with intarsia and duplicate stitch. Variegated yarn and bobbled trims add textural interest.

SIZES
Instructions are written for Man's or Woman's size Medium/ Large.

KNITTED MEASUREMENTS
▪ Bust or chest 42"/106.5cm
▪ Length 25"/63.5cm

MATERIALS
▪ 7 1¾oz/50g skeins (each approx 100yds/91m) of K1C2 *Parfait Swirls* (wool④) in #4555 multi (MC)
▪ 1 skein each in #1656 blue (A), #1730 purple (B), #1212 red (C) and #1526 green (D)
▪ One pair size 7 (4.5mm) needles *or size to obtain gauge*
▪ Stitch holders
▪ Five ¾"/20mm buttons

GAUGES
▪ 19 sts and 26 rows to 4"/10cm over St st using size 7 (4.5mm) needles.
▪ 18 sts and 25 rows to 4"/10cm over chart pat using size 7 (4.5mm) needles.
Take time to check gauges.

Notes
1 When changing colors, twist yarns on WS to prevent holes in work.
2 K1 selvage sts are worked at each end of every row and are not figured into the finished measurements.
3 On the placement diagram, 5 and 5b are worked in St st and snowflake motif is duplicate stitched using small snowflakes from chart 2.

Bobble Rib
(over an odd number of sts)

Make Bobble (MB)
[P1, k1] twice in same st—4 sts, then sl 2nd, 3rd and 4th sts over first st.

Rows 1 and 5 (RS) P1 *k1, p1; rep from * to end.

Rows 2, 4, and 6 *K1, p1; rep from *, end k1.

Row 3 P1, *k1, p1, MB, p1; rep from * to end.

BACK
With MC, cast on 99 sts. Work 6 rows bobble rib. K 2 rows B, k 2 rows D. Change to MC and work in St st until piece measures 16"/40.5cm from beg, end with a RS row.

Armhole shaping
Bind off 7 sts at beg of next 2 rows, 2 sts at beg of next 2 rows, 1 st at beg of next 8 rows—73 sts. Work even until armhole measures 8½"/21.5cm. K 2 rows A, k 2 rows D. Place sts on holder.

LEFT FRONT

With MC, cast on 49 sts. Work 6 rows bobble rib. K 2 rows B, k 2 rows D, dec 1 st on last WS row.

Beg chart pat

Row 1 (RS) K1 (selvage st), work in St st, foll schematic diagram for chart placement, end k1 (selvage st). Cont as established until piece measures 16"/40.5cm from beg.

Neck and armhole shaping

Next row (RS) Work to last 3 sts, k2tog, k1. Work 1 row even. Cont to dec 1 st at neck edge every other row twice more, every 4th row 11 times, AT SAME TIME, shape armhole at beg of RS rows as for back—21 sts. Work even until armhole measures 8½"/21.5cm. K 2 rows B, k 2 rows D. Place sts on holder.

RIGHT FRONT

Work to correspond to left front, foll placement diagram for right front, reversing all shaping and working neck shaping as foll: K1, SKP, work to end.

FINISHING

Block pieces to measurements. Foll charts for embroidery. With MC, duplicate stitch a 4 st x 4 st square at corners of blocks. Using 3 needle bind off method, bind off shoulder seams.

Front Band

With RS facing and C, pick up and k 86 sts to top of 2nd block, pm, 44 sts along neck edge, 31 sts from back neck holder, 44 sts along neck edge to top of 2nd block, pm, 86 sts along right front—291 sts. K 1 row. K 2 rows A. Change to MC and k 1 row, then work 1 row in k1, p1 rib.

Next (buttonhole) row Rib 3, *bind off 3 sts, rib 17 sts; rep from * 3 times more, bind off 3 sts, rib to end. Cast on 3 sts over the bound-off sts on next row and work bobbles around neck between markers. Rib 2 rows more. Bind off in rib.

Armhole bands

With RS facing and B, pick up and k 101 sts around armholes. K 1 row. K 2 rows D. Change to MC and k 1 row. Then work 5 rows in bobble rib. Bind off in rib. Sew side and armhole band seams.

Sew on buttons.

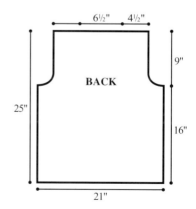

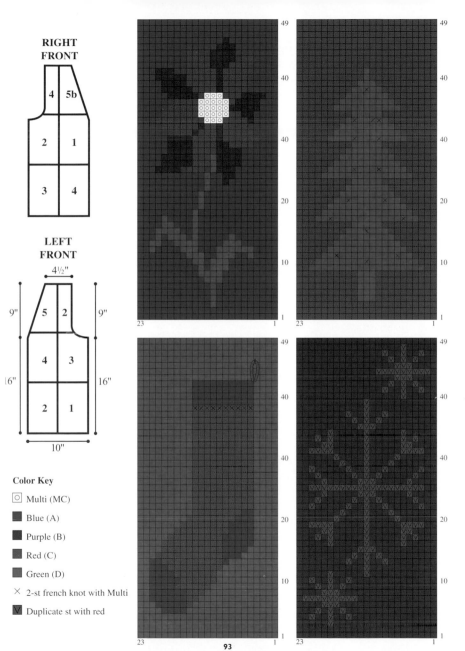

RIGHT FRONT

4	5b
2	1
3	4

LEFT FRONT

4½"

5	2
4	3
2	1

9" 9"

16" 16"

10"

Color Key

⊙ Multi (MC)

■ Blue (A)

■ Purple (B)

■ Red (C)

■ Green (D)

✕ 2-st french knot with Multi

Ⅴ Duplicate st with red

RESOURCES

US RESOURCES

*Write to the yarn
companies listed below for
purchasing and mail-order
information.*

ANNY BLATT
7796 Boardwalk
Brighton, MI 48116

BARUFFA
distributed by
Lane Borgosesia

BAABAJOE'S WOOL COMPANY
PO Box 26064
Lakewood, CO 80226

BERROCO, INC.
PO Box 367
Uxbridge, MA 01569

BROWN SHEEP CO.
100662 County Road 16
Mitchell, NE 69357

BUTTONMAD
www.buttonmad.com

CHERRY TREE HILL YARN
PO Box 659
Barton , VT 05822

CLASSIC ELITE YARNS
300A Jackson Street
Lowell, MA 01852

DALE OF NORWAY, INC.
N16 W23390 Stoneridge Dr.
Suite A
Waukessha, WI 53188

FILATURA DI CROSA
distributed by
Tahki•Stacy Charles, Inc.

GGH
distributed by
Muench Yarns

JAEGER HANDKNITS
5 Northern Blvd.
Amherst, NH 03031

JCA
35 Scales Lane
Townsend, MA 01469

KIC2, LLC
2220 Eastman Ave. #105
Ventura, CA 93003

KOIGU WOOL DESIGNS
R.R. #1
Willamsford, ON N0H 2V0

LANE BORGOSESIA
PO Box 217
Colorado Springs, CO 80903

MISSION FALLS
distributed by
Unique Kolours

MUENCH YARNS
285 Bel Marin Keys Blvd.
Unit J
Novato, CA 94949-5724

NATURALLY
distributed by
S. R. Kertzer, Ltd.

PATONS®
PO Box 40
Listowel, ON N4W 3H3

REYNOLDS
distributed by
JCA

ROWAN YARNS
5 Northern Blvd.
Amherst, NH 03031

S. R. KERTZER, LTD.
105A Winges Road
Woodbridge, ON L4L 6C2
Canada

SCHOELLER ESSLINGER
distributed by
Skacel Collection, Inc.

**SKACEL COLLECTION,
INC.**
PO Box 88110
Seattle, WA 98138-2110

TAHKI•STACY CHARLES, INC.
1059 Manhattan Ave.
Brooklyn, NY 11222

TRENDSETTER YARNS
16742 Stagg Street
Suite 104
Van Nuys, CA 91406

UNIQUE KOLOURS
1428 Oak Lane
Downingtown, PA 19335

WOOL PAK YARNS NZ
distributed by
Baabajoe's Wool Company

WOOL IN THE WOODS
58 Scarlet way
Biglerville, PA 17307

CANADIAN RESOURCES

Write to US resources for mail-order availability of yarns not listed.

BERROCO, INC.
distributed by
S. R. Kertzer, Ltd.

CLASSIC ELITE YARNS
distributed by
S. R. Kertzer, Ltd.

DIAMOND YARN
9697 St. Laurent
Montreal, PQ H3L 2N1
and
155 Martin Ross, Unit #3
Toronto, ON M3J 2L9

ESTELLE DESIGNS & SALES, LTD.
Units 65/67
2220 Midland Ave.
Scarborough, ON M1P 3E6

FILATURA DI CROSA
distributed by
Diamond Yarn

KOIGU WOOL DESIGNS
R. R. #1
Williamsford, ON N0H 2V0

LES FILS MUENCH, CANADA
5640 Rue Valcourt
Brossard, Quebec J4W1C5

MUENCH YARNS
distributed by
Les Fils Muench, Canada

MISSION FALLS
PO Box 224
Consecon, ON K0K1T0

NATURALLY
distributed by
S. R. Kertzer, Ltd.

PATONS ®
PO Box 40
Listowel, ON N4W 3H3

ROWAN
distributed by
Diamond Yarn

S. R. KERTZER, LTD.
105A Winges Rd.
Woodbridge, ON L4L 6C2

SCHOELLER ESSLINGER
distributed by
S. R. Kertzer, Ltd.

UK RESOURCES

Not all yarns used in this book are available in the UK. For yarns not available, make a comparable substitute or contact the US manufacturer for purchasing and mail-order information.

ROWAN YARNS
Green Lane Mill
Holmfirth
West Yorks HD7 1RW
Tel: 01484-681881

SILKSTONE
12 Market Place
Cockermouth
Cumbria, CA13 9NQ
Tel: 01900-821052

THOMAS RAMSDEN GROUP
Netherfield Road
Guiseley
West Yorks LS20 9PD
Tel: 01943-872264

VOGUE KNITTING VESTS

Editor-in-Chief
TRISHA MALCOLM

Art Director
CHI LING MOY

Executive Editor
CARLA S. SCOTT

Contributing Editor
BETTY CHRISTIANSEN

Instructions Editors
KAREN GREENWALD
CHARLOTTE PARRY
MARI LYNN PATRICK

Schematics
CHARLOTTE PARRY

Knitting Coordinator
JEAN GUIRGUIS

Yarn Coordinator
VERONICA MANNO

Editorial Coordinator
MICHELLE LO

Photography
BOBB CONNORS

Book Manager
THERESA MCKEON

Production Manager
DAVID JOINNIDES

■

President, SOHO Publishing Company
ART JOINNIDES